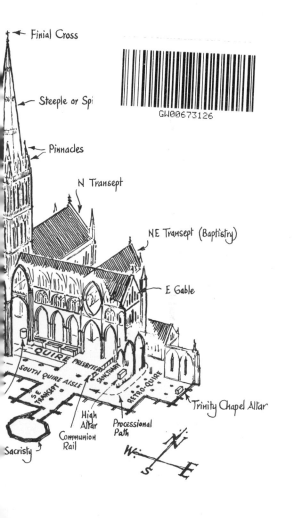

Finial Cross

Steeple or Spi

Pinnacles

N Transept

NE Transept (Baptistry)

E Gable

QUIRE

PRESBYTERY

SOUTH QUIRE AISLE

SANCTUARY

RETRO-QUIRE

S.E. TRANSEPT

High Altar

Processional Path

Communion Rail

Trinity Chapel Altar

Sacristy

Cranleigh
Monday 22nd May 1978

The Observer's Pocket Series

CATHEDRALS

The Observer Books

A POCKET REFERENCE SERIES

COVERING NATURAL HISTORY, TRANSPORT
THE ARTS ETC

The Observer's Book of
CATHEDRALS

ANTHONY S. B. NEW
F.S.A., F.R.I.B.A., M.I.Struct.E.

WITH 16 FULL-PAGE PLATES
AND OVER 250 ILLUSTRATIONS
IN COLOUR AND BLACK-AND-WHITE

FREDERICK WARNE & CO LTD
FREDERICK WARNE & CO INC
LONDON · NEW YORK

LIST OF PLATES

ISBN 0 7232 1500 6

Printed in Great Britain by
Lowe & Brydone (Printers) Ltd.
London

CONTENTS

PREFACE

More, perhaps, than with any other subject, a writer on cathedrals is humbled by the immense amount of literature already available and baffled by having to condense so many facts whilst at the same time trying to present them in a fresh way.

Amongst the friends who helped me with this absorbing task I am proud to record the names of my partners Mr Paul Paget C.V.O., F.S.A., F.R.I.B.A. and Mr Roy Rushton F.R.I.B.A., as well as those of Mr Alban Caroe F.S.A., F.R.I.B.A., Mr Anthony Chatwin F.R.I.B.A., Mr Peter Coard, Mr Sebastian Comper F.R.I.B.A., Mr Vincent Leaning, Mr Warwick Metcalfe, Mr George Pace F.S.A., F.R.I.B.A., Miss Judith Scott O.B.E., F.S.A., wardens and vergers at Bradford, Canterbury, Leicester, Lichfield, St Paul's, Wakefield and elsewhere who have given so freely of their time and knowledge, and Mr A. F. Kersting for providing photographs for plates A, C, E, G, H, J, L, Q.

I owe special gratitude to Mr Lawrence Jones, author of *The Observer's Book of Old English Churches*, for allowing me, if not actually to trespass on his ground, at any rate to approach it fairly closely. For further study I particularly commend his explanations of church fittings and furnishings. I am grateful to the publishers who, unruffled by the problems posed by my first book, *The Observer's Book of Postage Stamps*, allowed me to try their patience and skill with such a very different theme.

My greatest debt is to Elizabeth, who became my wife when the book was nearly ready for the printer. Her encouragement brought it to completion and many slips and obscurities were eradicated as a result of her painstaking criticism and proof-reading.

Despite the pressure of space, many abbeys, priories and collegiate churches are also included in the following pages, for to study cathedral architecture without at least glancing at monastic churches would be like exploring only one bank of a great river and ignoring the tributaries and landmarks on the other.

1 THE PURPOSE AND USE OF CATHEDRALS

A great cathedral is one of the mightiest, most sublime works of man. Few of us are unmoved by the rhythms and counter-rhythms of majestic columns and soaring vaults, the coloured harmonies of great traceried windows, the endless shapes and patterns of carvings in stone and wood, or the splendid climax of a bell-tower rising sheer from a green close, or seen at a distance above city roofs or water-meadows.

What is a cathedral and how does it differ from a church? Quite simply, a cathedral is a church which contains the seat or throne of a bishop (*94*) (Greek *cathedra*, seat). It is not a question of size. Westminster Abbey is not a cathedral, for there is nò Anglican bishop of Westminster. Yet the comparatively modest nine-teenth-century Roman Catholic church at Brentwood in Essex is one, having been raised to that status when the bishopric was created in 1917. Perhaps the smallest complete cathedral (though now superseded by a bigger building alongside it) is the tiny thirteenth-century one in Athens, which is only 38 feet long (*1*).

A bishop's territory of jurisdiction, of which he is prelate, is called a diocese. Sometimes the words see (from the Latin *sedes* for seat or throne) or episcopate

Athens Old Cathedral

1

7

are used instead of bishopric, and variants of these words may be recognized in other languages: *sé*, for example, is Portuguese for cathedral, and *esgob* is Welsh for bishop. A group of dioceses is a province with a metropolitan or archbishop at its head.

Here a few words are necessary about the various Churches. In the Middle Ages the Roman Catholic Church with a pope at its head held sway throughout most of Europe. By the early sixteenth century discontent and dissent had grown to such an extent that a number of sects broke away from it. These were called Protestants after the *Protestatio* of 1529 challenging the Diet of Speier which had sought to make plain the Church's immutibility.

In England the Reformation of religion culminated in Henry VIII's break with Rome and finally in the Act of Supremacy of 1559. Before 1535 all churches, monasteries and cathedrals had been Roman Catholic. In the course of four years the monasteries were dissolved and their wealth distributed, and the Church of England as we know it today came into being.

Henceforward those who held to the old faith and those who sought even newer ways of worship without bishops or cathedrals (Nonconformists) were subjected to varying degrees of persecution. It was not until 1829 that Roman Catholics were again permitted to worship freely. From then on, new Catholic dioceses were gradually established, so that one or two cities like Liverpool and Portsmouth now have both Anglican and Catholic cathedrals.

In the Latin countries (France, Spain, Italy, etc.) Roman Catholicism has on the whole been much less disturbed, and the cathedrals too. In Northern Europe, where Protestantism took a firmer hold, some of the sects such as the Lutherans and the Moravians have bishops, whilst other reformed churches do not. There, former cathedrals may sometimes be found renamed and

internally rearranged, like the Groote Kerk or Great
Church at Haarlem in Holland – a country where
Protestants and Catholics now live in approximately
equal numbers. In Scotland, more sadly, the Reformation led to the sacking of many fine cathedrals, like Elgin
(*171*, Pl. H) and Dunkeld (see p. 133).

Eastern Europe has the Eastern Orthodox Church,
which rejects papal authority (see p. 191). Other eastern
branches of Christianity include the Armenian and
Coptic Churches. This book, however, is chiefly concerned with cathedrals of the Anglican and Roman
Catholic Churches, and there is no space to digress
into the other forms of Christian worship.

To return, then, to bishops. We have seen that a
bishop is the head of a diocese, but what are his responsibilities ? Primarily he ordains priests, he confirms, he
celebrates Communion on certain occasions, he preaches
and appoints preachers, he presides at visitations and
synods, and he consecrates new churches. He also takes
on numerous other responsibilities, according to the
needs of his area and his own special interests – such as
committee work, writing, broadcasting and teaching. In
all this he may have an assistant bishop (possibly an
older man who has relinquished the responsibilities of a
diocese of his own) or suffragan bishop who deputizes
for him in parts of the diocese, and who takes his title
from some other important town.

Thus in all these activities (and many more) the
cathedral is regarded as the focal point; in it are celebrated not only the great festivals of the Church, but
also gatherings and thanksgivings of civic and industrial
organizations, the armed services, schools, women's
societies, professional bodies and many others from
all walks of life in the diocese. Some cathedrals, like
Trondhjem in Norway and, formerly, Reims in France,
are traditionally coronation churches, serving a similar
purpose to Westminster Abbey.

There is far more than this in the life of a cathedral and its diocese, and we must return to the subject later in this chapter. Enough has, however, been described to make it obvious that the bishop himself cannot possibly undertake the business affairs of the cathedral, quite apart from those of his entire diocese. We should remember, too, that all the senior bishops and the two archbishops in England have the ancient privilege and responsibility of sitting in Parliament.

In fact the management of a cathedral is the duty of the dean and chapter. The chapter consists of canons, a word applied to Church rules as well as to those officers who have to abide by them. The dean (originally meaning chief of ten) is the head of the chapter, and in what are called the Old Foundation cathedrals the chapter consists of three canons: the precentor (literally the first singer), the chancellor who directs the cathedral school (it is significant that this title is also used for the head of a university), and the treasurer. In the newer cathedrals these traditional titles are less frequently used, and the head of the chapter or cathedral council is sometimes the provost. A larger body, usually called the greater chapter, also comprises other canons (in Old Foundation cathedrals called prebendaries), who, although in charge of their own parishes, have special duties and are entitled to personal seats or stalls in the cathedral. A few cathedrals have lay canons – businessmen (and sometimes women) who are not clergy but who have a special interest in the work of the cathedral. The chapter clerk, usually a solicitor, sometimes also has his own stall.

The clergy who actually sing the services are usually deputies to the principal canons. In some older cathedrals they are still called vicars choral (though this term is now more often applied to lay choirmen) and they often have their own titles – the precentor's deputy the succentor (under-singer), the chancellor's the vice-chancellor and the treasurer's the sacrist (he is responsible for the

sacred treasures). They are also often called minor
canons and their duties include the daily Matins and
Evensong that are sung in the quire or choir.

Of the many other people who serve a cathedral – not
usually as clergy but as laymen – we must remember
the organist, the choirmen, sometimes also known as lay
vicars or lay clerks, the choirboys and their teachers
(cathedral choir schools are amongst the oldest in the
country), the bellringers, usually a purely voluntary
organization formed into a guild, the vergers or virgers
who carry a verge or poker to clear the way for processions, the subsacrists who assist the sacrist in the
collection of offerings and similar duties, the surveyor
who advises on building matters and is often called upon
to design fittings and ornaments, the clerk-of-works and
his staff who deal with day-to-day maintenance of the
fabric, the registrar who handles all the routine adminis-
tration, the librarian who may have the care of priceless
manuscripts and early books and documents, and last but
not least the secretaries, clerical staff, messengers,
watchmen and others who assist with essential tasks of
many kinds. All these are quite apart from the diocesan
organization, whose headquarters are usually to be
found close to the cathedral, and which deals with
financial, educational and many other matters of common concern to the parishes forming a diocese.

It may be helpful to mention certain others whose
duties do not necessarily connect them directly with
their cathedral, particularly archdeacons who are responsible to the bishop for groups of parishes called arch-
deaconries (usually about three to a diocese), rural deans
who have somewhat similar duties but towards smaller
groups (each archdeaconry comprises several rural
deaneries), and incumbents of single parishes (or sometimes of two or more adjacent ones) who may be either
rectors or vicars. A chaplain (literally a priest in charge
of a chapel) may nowadays be associated with a unit of

the forces or a civil organization. Each of the above may nevertheless also possess important responsibilities to his cathedral by being, to take two examples, a member of the chapter or a teacher at the choir school. A deacon is a man ordained to holy orders; his first appointment is generally that of curate or assistant to the incumbent of a parish.

The Roman Catholic Church does not normally have archdeacons; cardinals are members of its governing body, the College of Cardinals at Rome, and are usually bishops.

Cathedrals and monasteries frequently look so much alike that we must now digress just a little so as to understand their similarities and differences. Monasteries were, and are, of many kinds or orders. Basically, however, they are communities of men, or sometimes women, who devote their lives to worship and contemplation and to good works. Some, like the Carthusians, are enclosed, making little communication with the outside world. Others are specially concerned with missionary work, or education, or the care of the aged and infirm, and many of our oldest schools and hospitals owe their foundation to medieval monks. They also contributed widely to the early development of science, literature, art, architecture, agriculture and indeed to culture as a whole. The most important monasteries, called abbeys, have as their head an abbot (or abbess), but some quite large and many smaller ones are priories, with a prior (or prioress). Convents in England are houses of women (nuns), but the equivalent word in several other languages includes communities of men (monks) also.

The oldest order of monks is the Benedictine, founded by St Benedict in Italy in the sixth century. All the older English monasteries, like Westminster and Peterborough, were Benedictine, and their churches were usually planned with aisles and a square cloister, normally on the south side. The dormitory lay on the east

side of the cloister, so as to give easy access to the
church at all times, and the refectory (dining-hall) on
the south, that is furthest from the church (*113*). An
outer court, approached by a gatehouse, contained
stores, bakehouse, guest-house and, in the bigger establishments, many other domestic buildings.

Nearly all the orders founded subsequently began
with the object of interpreting the rules of St Benedict
more strictly, after the Benedictines and others had for
various reasons successively strayed somewhat from
them. The Cluniac, founded at Cluny in Burgundy in
940, built churches with double transepts (as later used
at Salisbury (*138*) and Lincoln (*121*)). The Cistercian,
founded at Cîteaux (also in Burgundy) in 1098, had
neither towers (Fountains Abbey (*154*) is an exception)
nor painted glass in its churches, which had short transepts and eastern arms, so that the quire often extended
westward of the crossing. The Augustinian, introduced
in England in 1105, was very like the Benedictine; its
churches include St Bartholomew the Great in London
and the cathedrals of Bristol (*104*), Carlisle (*107*) and
Oxford (*129*).

The Carthusian order, quite unlike the others, forbade speech entirely, providing each monk with a cell-
house adjoining a great cloister, where he worked, ate
and drank in solitary confinement, joining with his
fellows only in the church.

Then there were the military orders – the Knights
Templars and the Knights Hospitallers – which need
not concern us here.

Friars, itinerant preachers, often built large ·hall-
churches. The Dominicans (Black Friars) were founded
by St Dominic and the Franciscans (Grey Friars) by St
Francis of Assisi; the Carmelites (White Friars) were
driven from Mount Carmel by the Saracens in 1098 and
the Austin Friars were a hermit order, a union of various
movements. The Jesuits were founded much later, as

a counter-force to the Reformation.

Some cathedrals, such as Rochester (*134*), were monastic; that is, until the time of Henry VIII they were monasteries as well as being at the same time cathedral establishments in the sense we know today, a kind of dual role hardly met with outside England and Germany. They had a bishop at their head but were ruled by a prior, with similar responsibilities to a dean. Being refounded in the sixteenth century, they are sometimes called New Foundation, as distinct from the ancient non-monastic cathedrals like St Paul's which are Old Foundation. At the Reformation some purely monastic churches, like Peterborough (*131*), were also made cathedrals of completely new dioceses while some, such as Christchurch (*150*) and Pershore, were turned wholly or partly to parish use. But the great majority either fell gently to ruin, like Tintern, were plundered for their building material, like Reading, or were converted into mansions for the nobility, like Lacock in Wiltshire.

A further important class is the collegiate church, which was served by a college of priests, founded and endowed for a particular purpose. Some are grand buildings – like Beverley Minster (*149*), which has never been a cathedral, St George's Chapel, Windsor (*164*), a royal foundation governed by a dean and chapter as though it were a cathedral, and Southwell (*141*, Pl. A), which became a cathedral only in the nineteenth century.

Greater churches (whether collegiate or monastic) share with cathedrals so many similarities that it would be misleading to attempt any clear architectural distinction between those which possess a bishop's throne and those which do not. Much more rewarding is an examination of such cathedrals as Leicester (*119*) and Chelmsford (*108*) where the form of a parish church had to be ingeniously adapted to house its new functions.

But having now seen what those functions are, and who are concerned with them, we can look at the front endpaper and see how each part of a cathedral has its own purpose. The quire or choir* has the high altar as its focal point and contains the stalls of the canons and choir. Traditionally the chief canons have the corner stalls. The antiphonal mode of singing arises from (or gave rise to) the two banks of stalls facing one another; somewhere above them is the organ. Close by usually stands the bishop's throne (*94*) (see p. 70). On great occasions and for the main services the congregation occupies the nave, which is planned with aisles to allow processions to circulate, for example, clockwise around the east end and south aisle and finally up the centre towards the high altar. The transepts, north and south, may be used by additional congregation, but they developed also from the need to provide small chapels for private devotions, for masses for the dead, and for the cults of individual saints. Often a local saint held in particular esteem was buried east of the high altar, his shrine becoming a centre for pilgrimage: St Thomas à Becket's at Canterbury is the best known. In the thirteenth and fourteenth centuries a special veneration of the Virgin Mary led to the building of eastern Lady Chapels. The crossing is the square area where the transepts meet the nave and quire, usually capped by a central tower. In some cathedrals, however, (for instance Peterborough) the quire extends west of the crossing, only the presbytery, that is the immediate surroundings of the altar, with communion rail and seats for priests and perhaps some choir, being east of it. The cloisters are, of course, monastic in nature and origin (see p. 62) and usually provide access to the chapter house (see p. 64). The sacristy, near the east end, is a store for precious things like communion plate, whilst the vestries house the often equally precious robes, altar frontals and the like.

---

* Both spellings are correct. In this book quire is used for the part of the building and choir for those who sing in it.

2 STYLES OF ARCHITECTURE
(ENGLAND AND WALES)

The parcelling of architectural history into neatly labelled periods is unavoidable but can blind us to the evolutionary process of the styles. Sometimes an innovation, like the early pointed arches at Fountains or the Perpendicular tracery at Gloucester, can be exactly dated but characteristics of one style continually intermingle with those of the next, details are copied out of respect for original work or for less obvious reasons, and authorities differ on what exactly constitutes a change of style. Nevertheless the following names are universally applied to English architecture; the colours alongside are used wherever possible in this book to distinguish the styles (see p. 80):

SAXON for pre-Conquest work from the 7th c. till 1066

NORMAN for the round-arched style of 1066 until about 1190

EARLY ENGLISH for the first Gothic work of about 1140 to 1260

DECORATED for the middle Gothic of about 1250 to 1360 including the so-called Geometric

PERPENDICULAR for the late Gothic of about 1340 until as late as the 17th c.

RENAISSANCE for imitative Classical work, principally that of the late 16th c. up to the early 19th c.

VICTORIAN for 19th-c. work in imitative styles, mostly Gothic

MODERN CLASSICAL, MODERN GOTHIC for modern imitative styles. True non-derivative work of the 20th c. is left uncoloured (see p. 80)

SAXON, seventh century to 1066

To imagine the appearance of a typical English cathedral before the Conquest is not easy, for little survives except the tiny seventh-century crypt at Ripon.

The commonest traditional form of a church in the Roman Empire was a rectangle attached to a semi-circle or apse which housed the altar. Almost certainly this was derived from the Roman civic basilica. When such a building was a cathedral or monastic church, the part nearest the eastern apse was the quire, while the lay congregation used the further area. The extreme west end was sometimes raised to form a tower, or transepts were added as well, for instance at the ruined cathedral of North Elmham (*2*), to form a cross or cruciform plan. These two were, one supposes, smaller than the average in size. At Winchester the excavations of the Saxon cathedral (now reburied) lying to the north of the present one indicated a construction with side aisles rather akin to Brixworth church, Northamptonshire, the grandest building of these mysterious centuries remaining to us.

The architectural details that there were came mostly from Roman sources, imperfectly understood: round arches with a minimum of ornamental moulding, little columns with quite elementary caps and bases, triangular heads to the smaller openings, the pairing of windows with a baluster between (*3*), and the application of pilasters or strips of stone either to punctuate walls or to imitate timber structures of a kind long disappeared.

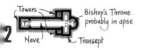

Plan of North Elmham Cathedral (to same scale as other plans on pages 81; etc.) c. 1000

Tower window, Deerhurst Priory

NORMAN, 1066 to *circa* 1190

The earliest post-Conquest cathedrals of which substantial portions remain are St Alban's and Winchester, the quire aisles of Gloucester, the crypt of Worcester (*91*) and the nucleus of Lincoln's west front.

The apse-ended plan form with transepts continued to be developed, from the quite simple type excavated at Old Sarum to designs of great complexity. At the same time, however, the square type of east end (by no means unknown before the Conquest) continued to be built, as at Romsey Abbey (*158*). Here there is a processional way behind the altar. Often as again at Romsey, each transept also had one or two apses on its east side forming minor chapels. At Canterbury (*106*) and elsewhere, a second transept was built, east of the main one.

Nearly all apsidal east ends were provided with a processional aisle right round, the columns and arches usually maintaining the semi-circular plan form as in Peterborough (*131*) and Norwich (*128*). Against this outer ambulatory were sometimes built more little chapels which were themselves semi-circular, the whole eastern grouping so formed being called a chevet. The use of a French word rightly suggests that such a plan is commoner in France than in England. The least altered English example is at Norwich (*128*, Pl. B).

A short quire meant that the stalls had to extend past the crossing into an elongated nave, an illogical arrangement which persists for instance at St Alban's.

Great towers were often built over crossings, at Winchester (*145*), for instance, and equally often also at west ends, either singly as at Ely (*114*) or in pairs as at Southwell (*141*, Pl. A). They also occurred in positions later regarded as rather odd: over the transepts (Exeter, *115*), adjoining eastern transepts (Canterbury, *106*) or even over the quire aisles as once existed at Hereford.

The earliest church arcades, at St Alban's, for example, sometimes look as though they were hewn from a solid wall, and in smaller buildings some probably were. Aisles would be built alongside an earlier nave and when the roofs were weathertight a series of openings would be knocked through the dividing walls, leaving great piers of masonry to be roughly squared up and plastered. Typical Norman piers or columns, however, are circular (*6*) or clustered (*4*) and occasionally enriched with incised patterns (*7*). Their bases are quite simple, often square (*7*), and the capitals nearly always follow some variant of the 'cushion' (*14*) or 'scalloped' form (*7, 9, 13*) – except where specially skilled sculptors had a hand (*12*). About 1170 there appeared a distinctive kind of capital called the 'water-leaf' (*15*).

In different buildings varying relative degrees of importance were given to the main arcade, the tribune or triforium gallery (usually with windows) and the clerestory (above the aisle roofs lighting the upper part of the nave). Sometimes, as in the quire of Norwich, the gallery is as high as the main arcade below. Conversely the clerestory and triforium could be treated together as virtually one unit subservient to the giant arcade, at Tewkesbury Abbey and Gloucester (*6*) for instance. Designers exercised their ingenuity too in the punctuation of the overall pattern of openings by means of vertical shafts and horizontal string courses, and explored many different ways of grouping small openings within larger.

Many of the most splendid Norman churches never had anything more ambitious than a flattish timber ceiling, but originally these were richly painted and gilded, as at Ely. Stone vaults were almost always quadripartite, i.e. square or nearly square on plan and, in effect, two intersecting semi-cylinders (*5*). Ribs began to be introduced for strength (*4*) and as an aid to assembly. Early vaults without ribs are called 'groined' (*9*).

AISLE VAULTING RIBS

THE NAVE HAS A FLAT WOOD CEILING

ROLL MOULDINGS

CLERESTORY

SCALLOPED CAPITALS

ZIGZAG MOULDING

TRIBUNE OR GALLERY

SHAFTS OF CLUSTERED PIER

PIER

SEMICIRCULAR ARCHES

4
NAVE ARCADES
PETERBOROUGH
c. 1160

NAVE ARCADE

NAVE PIER BASE

AISLE

5   c. 1080
EARLY QUADRIPARTITE VAULT
WINCHESTER N. TRANSEPT

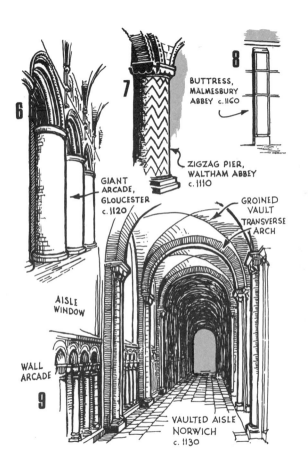

6 GIANT ARCADE, GLOUCESTER c.1120

7 ZIGZAG PIER, WALTHAM ABBEY c.1110

8 BUTTRESS, MALMESBURY ABBEY c.1160

GROINED VAULT

TRANSVERSE ARCH

AISLE WINDOW

WALL ARCADE

9 VAULTED AISLE NORWICH c.1130

The principal characteristics of Norman building, apart from the almost universal use of the semi-circular arch, are massiveness and dignity, with a reliance on sheer weight rather than niceties of thrust and balance.

Because walls were so thick and heavy, there was little need for buttresses; these, when provided, were quite shallow projections serving as architectural punctuations rather than supports (8). Central towers (i.e. over the crossing) may have been preferred on account of the extra strength gained by the stabilizing effect of the walls of the list of such towers that collapsed is formidably long. Walls are not always as solid as they seem, and often two skins of fine stonework conceal a core of rubble or rubbish or even extensive voids!

Windows are quite small, and almost always round-headed. Often, as before the Conquest, they were built as twin openings with a baluster between. This duplex system of design also occurs on a far larger scale in many great arcades, such as Durham (113), where huge round piers alternate with even bigger composite ones, breaking up the overall design into a few large double bays instead of many single ones. Coloured glass was a rarity, and lesser buildings usually only had shutters.

Doorways also are round-headed, but frequently the top semi-circle is filled by a carved stone tympanum. The more important openings were built up in two, three or more diminishing and receding arches or 'orders', each resting on its own little column or enriched with a continuation of the arch ornament (11).

By the late twelfth century external walls were frequently enriched with row upon row of surface arcading, in which actual openings were formed as necessary and the remainder left blind (10, 17). The low arcading often found at the base of walls, inside and out (9), is perhaps a relic, rather meaninglessly repeated, of the loggias of timber construction. Similarly the rows of corbels at the tops of walls (Pl. B), often elaborated into parades of grotesque heads, were probably derived from the modillioned cornices of classical architecture (*76*).

The round arches of the Saxon and Norman styles (together known as English Romanesque) should not be confused with those of the Renaissance (*76*); a glance at the mouldings and ornament will always reveal the difference. In fact, so far as can be judged from the few surviving remains, Saxon and early Norman buildings had little in the way of ornament. Yet by the middle of the twelfth century builders had an urge, even obsession, to cover every square foot of wall surface with some decoration or other. It is this development, as much as the gradual acquisition of skills in vaulting and in the design of arcades, that often enables the student to date the parts of a building to within a decade. The most common ornament is the zigzag (*16*), with its variants the chevron and rhombus. That and the interlaced or intersecting arcade (*10*) were first used as surface decorations quite early in the twelfth century. A number of other repeating ornaments are also typical of the period: the billet (a series of raised rectangles, sometimes forming a checker pattern) (*17*), the key (*11*), the cable and several kinds of diaper and interwoven patterns (*10*). The particular kind of grotesque head called a beak-head, because of its extended beak or beard which often seems to wrap round a roll-moulding, occurs almost *ad nauseam* (*16*).

The meaning of much Norman sculpture is lost to modern eyes. No one can really disentangle the involvement with legend, pagan mythology and religious conviction, from the experiences and whims of the individual artist-craftsman. The best is uninhibited art of the highest quality with strong undertones of the Celtic and Saxon cultures which had gone before (*12*).

INTERWOVEN ZIGZAG

INTERSECTING ARCADE

ALTERNATING PLAIN AND
SPIRAL-FLUTED COLUMNS

10

SHALLOW NICHES WITH
BLANK ARCHES

INTERNAL WALL OF
CHAPTER HOUSE
BRISTOL
c. 1160

STONE SEAT

ZIGZAG

KEY ORNAMENT

11
SOUTH DOORWAY
LLANDAFF c. 1170

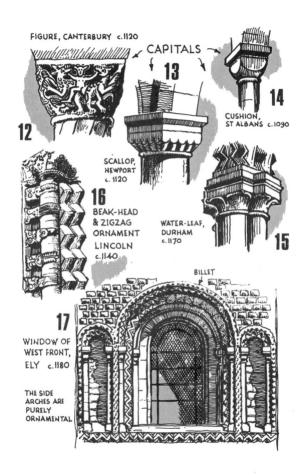

FIGURE, CANTERBURY c.1120

CAPITALS

13

14

CUSHION,
ST ALBANS c.1090

12

SCALLOP,
NEWPORT
c.1120

16

BEAK-HEAD
& ZIGZAG
ORNAMENT
LINCOLN
c.1140

WATER-LEAF,
DURHAM
c.1170

15

BILLET

17

WINDOW OF
WEST FRONT,
ELY c.1180

THE SIDE
ARCHES ARE
PURELY
ORNAMENTAL

EARLY ENGLISH, *circa* 1140 to 1260

The word Gothic, meaning the pointed-arch style, began as a term of derision during the time of the Renaissance of classical architecture indicating 'barbaric'. Of course the introduction of the pointed arch was not a sudden happening before which all was round-arched and afterwards all Gothic. The transition was a phase that has sometimes been regarded as a style in itself – Transitional Norman (or even just Transitional) – though it is easier to understand it as a medley of two styles than as a fusion; from this we can see why the abandonment of the Romanesque arch took place.

The early quadripartite vault (5) with its intersecting semi-cylinders was really only suited to the covering of square compartments. If the width of the nave was less than the spacing of the columns it was clearly impossible for both semi-cylinders to rise to the same height. However, when the smaller one was distorted to a pointed form, then the ridges or crowns of the vault could become level (20). Very soon it was realized that the semi-circular arch was an unnecessary impediment to design. There was no reason why both semi-cylinders should not be pointed in shape, nor why the arches of the clerestory, the gallery and the main arcades, the windows and the doorways should not be pointed too. Thus all the arches in a row could look the same height even if the columns had to vary in their spacing.

To what extent the change was accelerated by accounts brought back from the Crusades of Byzantine pointed arches will never be known. But it is certain that the Gothic style began rather earlier in France (p. 144) and that its true beginnings in England were due to the Cistercians (p. 13).

Typical instances of Transitional work are pointed arches on scalloped capitals as in Malmesbury Abbey (18) or, conversely, Gothic leaf capitals on Norman forms as in St Mary's Chapel, Glastonbury, and round arches intermingled with pointed as in the extraordinary westernmost nave bays of Worcester (*19*).

The increasing need of new chapels, places for shrines and better processional ways led to more and more eastward extensions. In older cathedrals, like Ely (*114*), the quire was rebuilt on a more lavish scale and when it was complete the apse-ended Norman quire, which had become increasingly inadequate for services, was taken down. A piecemeal appearance often results from such growth – stage by stage as needs arose and funds dictated – and tends to distinguish English cathedrals from their continental counterparts. Even at Salisbury, where the entire cathedral was planned afresh about 1220, the components are just as clearly and individually defined (*138*): long, rather narrow nave and aisles, long quire and aisles, long transepts now double and a grand eastern chapel.

In France the change to Gothic meant an appreciable lightening of construction – thinner walls and a clear expression of the transfer of vault-thrusts by means of buttresses (*182*). In England what we now call the Early English style (sometimes First Pointed, Early Gothic or Lancet) tended to be regarded rather more as an improved means of decoration. The nave arcades of Wells (*22*) are really only a little less heavy than those of, say, Chichester thirty or forty years earlier, and owe much of their beauty to a more delicate surface treatment.

Long, low outlines and squat towers are characteristic of the period; Salisbury, though it is hard to imagine now, had a low crossing-tower at first, which was certainly not intended to carry the great steeple added a century later. In spite of the verticality of lancet windows, horizontal lines and rhythms predominate (Pl. D).

West fronts began to be thought of as screens for the display of sculpture, as at Wells, or as *tours de force* of architectural display (Peterborough).

[LATER CLERESTORY NOT SHOWN]

TRIFORIUM STANDARD NORMAN

CLERESTORY
ROUND ARCH
BETWEEN TWO
POINTED

TRIFORIUM
THREE ROUND
ARCHES WITH
ZIGZAG, WITHIN
POINTED ARCH

ARCADE
POINTED ARCH
ON SHAFTED
PIERS

ARCADE
STANDARD NORMAN
EXCEPT FOR
POINTED ARCH

18 TRANSITIONAL NORMAN ARCADES **19**

MALMESBURY ABBEY c. 1165   WORCESTER c. 1185

DIAGRAM OF VAULT
OVER NON-SQUARE
COMPARTMENT

20 POINTED   ROUND

SHOWING ADVANTAGE
OF POINTED ARCH TO
ACHIEVE UNIFORM
RIDGE HEIGHT

TIERCERON
NAVE
VAULT

CLERESTORY

AISLE
VAULTING
RIBS

TRIFORIUM

DIAGRAM OF
EQUILATERAL ARCH

STIFF-LEAF CAPITAL

SPANDRELS

21

CLUSTERED
COLUMN
WITH PURBECK
MARBLE SHAFTS

AISLE
VAULT

SHAFT
BAND OR
RING

NAVE
ARCADE

NAVE
ARCADES
LINCOLN
c.1220

COLUMN
BASE

WALL ARCADE

NAVE

AISLE

Even the richest early Gothic columns are really quite simple forms on to which shafts have been added. At Wells (*22*) the basic section is a cross with a group of three shafts on each arm and in each hollow. All over England these decorative shafts were very frequently made of so-called Purbeck marble, a dark shelly limestone from Dorset. As the available lengths were limited, the joints in the longer shafts were masked by rings of stone (*21*) or, more rarely, copper. Large plain circular (*24*) and polygonal main columns were used at Canterbury and are common in smaller buildings.

The most usual types of capital are the so-called stiff-leaf, which resembles no natural form, and the delicately moulded inverted bell (*23*), but the range is quite considerable, from naturalistic carvings to the exclusion of ornament in buildings under the Cistercians (*25*).

Arch mouldings are usually at least as rich as their supporting columns, and may consist of a succession of deep rounded folds and hollows. Whilst in main arches an equilateral shape (*21*) is normal, a great variety of forms can be found in subsidiary arches (especially in triforia) from very pointed lancets to depressed, nearly round shapes and almost triangular forms.

The galleries over aisles became reduced in size to mere roof-spaces screened by the triforium arcades. Bay design, the detail and relationship of arcade, triforium and clerestory, reached its zenith of self-assurance and purity during this period.

The early vaults were still quadripartite, like a four-ribbed umbrella centred over each bay (*20*), though exceptional instances of sexpartite roofs in the French manner exist (*26*). Later, additional ribs called tiercerons were introduced, so that the impression became one of branches spreading palm-like from above each column and the eye thus reads a rhythm half a bay out of step with that of the columns (*27*). Salisbury, however, reverted to a simple quadripartite vault.

Walls were still thick enough to need only a minimum of buttressing (*34*), and the thrusts of high vaults could be carried within the structure of the aisle roofs.

Windows were seldom more than single pointed lights (lancets) or combinations of them. Some of these groups, like the west front of Ripon and the famous Five Sisters of York, are grand conceptions. Variety was achieved by grading their height (*35*) or by introducing smaller openings above, forming what is called plate tracery (*36*). Wheel windows, sometimes used by the Normans, were developed into grand rose windows (*30*). Glass, of which Canterbury has by far the most substantial surviving examples, took on new majesty with deep reds and blues. Salisbury was designed for the display of grisaille, a greyish patterned glass.

Cusps were introduced into all kinds of smaller arches; these pointed projections formed by intersecting curves gave Gothic masons a new rich vocabulary of shapes: trefoil- and cinquefoil-headed arches (*33*) and the range of foliated circles (*28, 29, 31, 32*) which was to be the basis of so-called Geometric Decorated, the next phase of design.

The usual embellishment of windows and doorways (*37*) was one or more shafts of Purbeck marble or other stone, moulded and carved like the columns of arcades. Wall-arcading sometimes appears in a double form with one rich line of shafts and arches well forward from a second blind row on the actual wall-face (Pl. C).

The favourite ornament was the dog-tooth in various forms (*38*). Far more important was the splendid development of sculpture – foliage and figure-carving, of which grievously little remains after later iconoclasm. Roof bosses, the knobbly pieces of stone that cover the intersections of vaulting ribs, were inaccessible to the hands of destroyers and have fared much better; but often their intricate detail, carved as a work of sheer joy, is invisible to the naked eye.

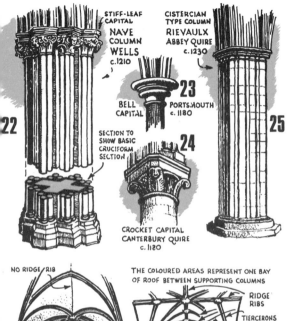

STIFF-LEAF CAPITAL
NAVE COLUMN
WELLS
c.1210

CISTERCIAN TYPE COLUMN
RIEVAULX ABBEY QUIRE
c.1230

BELL CAPITAL
PORTSMOUTH
c.1180

23

SECTION TO SHOW BASIC CRUCIFORM SECTION

24

22

25

CROCKET CAPITAL
CANTERBURY QUIRE
c.1120

NO RIDGE RIB

SIX RIBS OVER TWO BAYS WITH ONE CENTRAL BOSS ONLY

26

SEXPARTITE VAULT c.1180
CANTERBURY N·E TRANSEPT

THE COLOURED AREAS REPRESENT ONE BAY OF ROOF BETWEEN SUPPORTING COLUMNS

RIDGE RIBS

TIERCERONS

DIAGONAL RIBS

27

TIERCERON VAULT c.1250
ELY QUIRE

Plate A *Southwell, Norman west front. (The large window is a Perpendicular insertion.)*

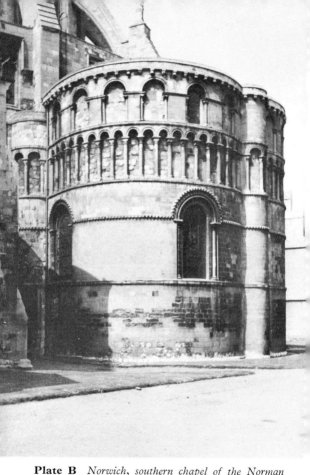

Plate B *Norwich, southern chapel of the Norman chevet showing typical wall arcade and corbels.*

Plate C *Lincoln, double wall arcade in the south quire aisle, Early English.*

Plate D *Salisbury, interior looking west, pure Early English.*

Plate E *Exeter, interior looking east, pure Decorated.*

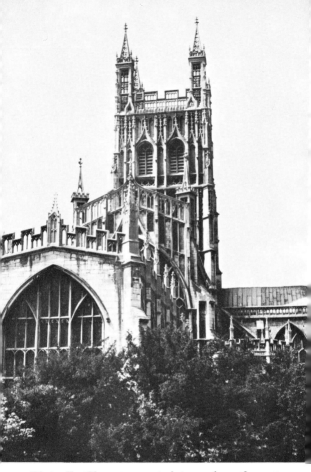

Plate F *Gloucester, central tower from the east, Perpendicular.*

Plate G *St Paul's, London, north west tower, Renaissance.*

Plate H *Elgin, Scotland, the south aisle, facing west.*

Plate J *Amiens, France, interior looking east, typical
French Middle Gothic.*

Plate K
Nebbio,
Corsica,
west front of
the Cathedral
in the
Vineyards,
simple early
Romanesque.

Plate L
Chartres, the west door showing stylized carving, French Early Gothic.

Plate M *Aix-en-Provence, France, early Romanesque baptistry with true Corinthian columns.*

Plate N *Angoulême, France, late Romanesque west front, early twelfth century.*

Plate O
*Segovia,
Spain, early
sixteenth
century.*

Plate P
Pisa, Italy, baptistry and cathedral from top of Leaning Tower, mostly twelfth century, but upper parts fourteenth century.

Plate Q
Cologne, Germany, from the south.

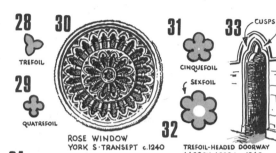

28 TREFOIL

29 QUATREFOIL

30 ROSE WINDOW
YORK S·TRANSEPT c.1240

31 CINQUEFOIL

32 SEXFOIL

33 CUSPS
TREFOIL-HEADED DOORWAY
LACOCK ABBEY c.1240

34 BUTTRESS
SALISBURY
NAVE AISLE
c.1240

35 STEPPED LANCETS
BRECON E.WINDOW
c.1210

36 BLIND
LOZENGE
BEGINNINGS
OF TRACERY:
CHAPTER HOUSE
LINCOLN c.1230

37 'Y' TRACERY
WITH BLIND SPANDREL
WORCESTER
QUIRE TRIFORIUM
c.1230

38 DOG-TOOTH ORNAMENT

39 SPRINGING
FOLIAGE
ORNAMENT

D

DECORATED, *circa* 1250 to 1360

Decorated is perhaps the least easy style to define and its alternative names Second Pointed and Middle Gothic certainly do not help. The more we examine it, the more we shall feel that it is not one style but many. The change from Norman to Early English (Early Gothic) has been likened to the coming of spring, when everything becomes more delicate and graceful. By the same analogy Decorated was the summer of English Gothic, when all the essential problems of structure had been solved and the art of ornament reached its highest peak; it signalled the start of an age of prosperity cut short in 1348 by the Black Death.

We should now pause to examine Westminster Abbey at the very point of transition from Early English to Decorated. It was never a cathedral except for a brief period in the sixteenth century, but it had enormous influence on major church building for many years. Because it was under royal patronage and because King Henry III loved all things French, it reflected French form and details – especially from Amiens, Paris and Reims cathedrals, the abbey of St Denis, and the Sainte-Chapelle in Paris. Obvious instances are the eastern chevet (the series of radiating polygonal chapels), the great height of the vault, the bar window-tracery, as well as a particular type of spherical triangle window design (*47*), the flying buttresses and several details of carved ornament such as angels in the arch-spandrels (*52*). Apart from the high vault and buttresses, and the chevet, which generally found no favour in England, these were extensively admired and copied.

Cloisters were sometimes added even to non-monastic cathedrals (Chichester, Salisbury, Wells) where they were hardly used except for processions.

Towers always culminated in spires of wood or stone: many of these tall steeples have disappeared, as from

Hereford and Lincoln.

Most remarkable of all the characteristics of Decorated was a striving after spatial effects: the subtle inter-penetrations of the quire and the retro-quire and the Lady Chapel at Wells, the fascinating stone engineering of the vaults of Bristol (*44*), and the overwhelmingly daring octagon hanging over the central crossing of Ely – to name but three.

Columns and arcades tended towards greater and greater multiplication of shafts and mouldings, though these clung closer to the stonework than the often detached shafts of the previous century. Capitals became less formal in their foliage designs, and much more free and naturalistic. The ogee arch with double reversed curves (*53*) was introduced, more particularly in win-dows, doorways and smaller details. In work of special richness the nodding arch, in which the top projects further forward than the remainder, appeared (*45*).

Vaults, too, became more and more luxuriant with their profusion of bosses and ribs. The greatest number of ribs in one cluster of a plain tierceron vault was eleven (Exeter, *40*, Pl. E), but as a further complexity lierne ribs were introduced. These do not spring from the same point as the main system but knit it together overhead to break the surface into smaller, more man-ageable areas for infilling (*42, 43*).

Whilst the clerestory remained essential for lighting the nave, the triforium, having ceased altogether to be the façade of the useless space over the aisle vaults, tended to become merged into it.

Walls continued to be fairly thick, but there often seems to have been a conflict of purpose between ex-pressing this thickness by, for instance, two layers of arcading (as in Early English, Pl. C) and, conversely, treating the decoration as surface-panelling (as in fifteenth-century Perpendicular work, *57*).

In each of the medieval styles window tracery is the

TIERCERON
NAVE VAULT

CLERESTORY

TRIFORIUM

NAVE
ARCADE

AISLE
VAULTING
RIBS

MOULDED
CAPITAL

40

CLUSTERED
COLUMN

NAVE
ARCADES
EXETER
c. 1310

COLUMN BASE

NAVE

AISLE

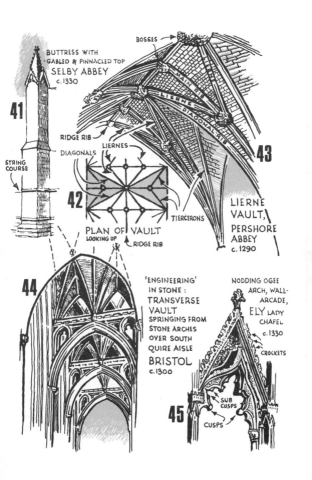

41 BUTTRESS WITH GABLED & PINNACLED TOP SELBY ABBEY c.1330

STRING COURSE

BOSSES

LIERNE

DIAGONAL RIB

43 LIERNE VAULT, PERSHORE ABBEY c.1290

RIDGE RIB

DIAGONALS LIERNES

42 PLAN OF VAULT LOOKING UP

RIDGE RIB

TIERCERONS

44

'ENGINEERING' IN STONE : TRANSVERSE VAULT SPRINGING FROM STONE ARCHES OVER SOUTH QUIRE AISLE BRISTOL c.1300

NODDING OGEE ARCH, WALL-ARCADE, ELY LADY CHAPEL c.1330

CROCKETS

45 SUB CUSPS

CUSPS

most readily identifiable feature, though in cathedrals
more than in any other buildings we have to be wary
of later alterations that often obscure the true dates of
the structure. Decorated windows inserted into Norman
walls for the purpose of admitting more light may make
the building itself look Decorated – until we look more
closely at the mouldings, buttresses and other details.

Decorated tracery is divided into two main groups,
Geometric and Curvilinear. Geometric is the style of
much of Westminster Abbey and of the buildings
derived from it (*46, 47*). Sometimes it is regarded as the
culminating phase of Early English, but if we remember
how much it owes to the French ideas introduced at
Westminster we shall probably agree with those who
regard it as the beginning of a new style, which later
developed into an original and wholly insular art form.

Geometric tracery, a grouping of cusped circles
(trefoils, quatrefoils, etc., *28*, etc.) within the pointed
head of a single window, is the earliest kind of bar
tracery, as opposed to plate tracery which had been in
effect a series of separate piercings of a solid wall (*36*).
From its mathematical precision it derives a curiously
rigid kind of elegance (*46*).

Curvilinear tracery was a reaction from this standardization. Here the designer had freer play and the mason
had to master the intricacies of setting out his pieces of
stone on curves struck from dozens of different centres
and radii. Patterns like the east windows of Selby Abbey
and of Carlisle (*48*), and the famous 'Bishop's Eye' of
Lincoln are sheer masterpieces. Less inventive designers
fell back on reticulated (net) tracery, composed of repeating identical units and adaptable to windows of two,
three, four or more main lights (*49*).

Glass, of which little remains even at York, began to
exhibit the elongated figures in canopies which were to
become so typical of the fifteenth century.

Doorway mouldings became more complex and lively;

richer ones have ogee heads, or saints in niches (*50, 51*).

Decorated ornament was a blossoming of naturalism between the stiffness of Early English and the formality of Perpendicular. Plants of the hedgerow (*56*), animals, saints and even sinners (such as the well-known apple-stealing scenes at Wells) were carved with a love and warmth that were not to reappear for more than three centuries. Just as marvellous was the skill with which this sculpture was integrated with the architecture, giving emphasis at just those points where it was needed and enhancing the richness and interplay of the mouldings.

In the Curvilinear phase ornament was even more lavishly applied, and entire buildings were treated almost as though they were organic forms. The interior of Exeter (*40*) has been likened to an avenue of stately trees whose branches (the main ribs and tiercerons of the vault) interlace overhead, while the mullions of a window of Dorchester Abbey actually take the form of branches, framing a series of stained glass panels which make up of a Tree of Jesse. One formalized ornament specially characteristic of the early fourteenth century is the so-called ball-flower, with which window and doorway mouldings were frequently encrusted (*54*).

Throughout medieval times churches and their furnishings were extensively coloured; ironwork was gilded, plain walls embellished with paintings, and carved stonework tinted in colours which today we might regard as garish. Nearly all this colour is now faded and gone.

Some of the most splendid Decorated craftsmanship is in monuments, especially in the little chantries set up and endowed so that priests could say masses for the dead for ever. 'For ever' ended with the Reformation, when many were plundered for their valuables, but we can still admire their small-scale architectural detail at. say, Salisbury, Hereford or Beverley Minster.

WINDOW TRACERY

46

GEOMETRIC

EAST WINDOW, LINCOLN c.1260

47

SPHERICAL TRIANGLE LICHFIELD c.1260

48

EAST WINDOW CARLISLE c.1320

49

MULLIONS

CURVI-LINEAR

RETICULATED WELLS c.1300

50

CHAPTER HOUSE DOORWAY SALISBURY c.1280

51

c.1310

PRIOR'S DOORWAY NORWICH

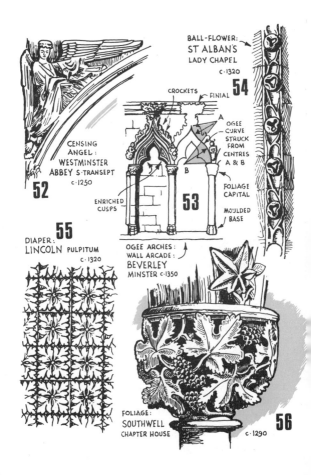

BALL-FLOWER:
ST ALBAN'S
LADY CHAPEL
c.1320

54

CENSING
ANGEL:
WESTMINSTER
ABBEY S·TRANSEPT
c·1250

52

CROCKETS   FINIAL

A
OGEE
CURVE
STRUCK
FROM
CENTRES
A & B

B

FOLIAGE
CAPITAL

MOULDED
BASE

ENRICHED
CUSPS

53

55

DIAPER:
LINCOLN PULPITUM
c·1320

OGEE ARCHES:
WALL ARCADE:
BEVERLEY
MINSTER c·1350

FOLIAGE:
SOUTHWELL
CHAPTER HOUSE

c·1290

56

PERPENDICULAR, *circa* 1340 to seventeenth century

The Perpendicular style is peculiar to England, but rather sparsely represented amongst her major churches: the only complete ones, all in some sense royal foundations, are Bath Abbey, King's College Chapel, Cambridge, and St George's Chapel, Windsor – none of them cathedrals. To see it in profusion we must turn to lesser works, for by the late Middle Ages merchants who had acquired great wealth were devoting it to civic buildings and town churches, whereas cathedrals on the whole were complete and secure. Nevertheless quite extensive changes were wrought at Gloucester (Pl. F), York, Canterbury (*57*), Winchester (*59*) and Norwich, and many cloisters and towers were added or rebuilt elsewhere.

Critics have rightly pointed out that the word Rectilinear would have been better than Perpendicular. It would express the horizontals as well as the repeating verticals – the window transoms, the rigid sub-divisions of wall panelling, the comparative flatness of the later vaults and arches, and the often monotonously repetitive rhythms of windows and buttresses along the façades.

So far as we know, the quire at Gloucester (*c.* 1330) is the oldest surviving Perpendicular building. It was, however, too suddenly perfect not to have had antecedents – though none of these exist today. In essence it is a delicate web of tracery thrown over the old Norman walls and arches, carried upwards high above and across them with a bafflingly complex vault, and left virtually open on the entire east end for a window the size of a tennis-court. The shape of the resulting space – crisply defined and awe-inspiring and completely abandoning the subtleties of Decorated – was to become typical of Late Gothic in England.

Structures became lighter in every respect: columns more slender, arches wider, walls thinner, windows bigger, in fact every part expressing more clearly the gathering of loads and thrusts all the way from the ridge of the roof down to the foundations of the walls.

The development of vaults in the new style was hesitant. Gloucester's quire vault does not really fit the disciplined construction beneath. The lierne roofs of Winchester (59) (also an encasing of a Norman structure) and of Tewkesbury Abbey have lost the earlier purity of structural expression and are more like intersecting barrel vaults with applied decoration. One problem that worried those who tried to rationalize these forms was that in principle all the tiercerons and the main ribs, the 'palm branches', had to be of different lengths. The solution, evolved at first on a very small scale (probably in the Despencer Chantry at Tewkesbury) and presently applied to cloisters, was to make all the branches identical, so that they formed a semi-circular fan (60). The advantage of this standardization had to be weighed against the difficulty of supporting the flat four-sided pieces between the fans at the top. In the larger vaults the fans either had to be spaced apart and vaulted between, as at Sherborne Abbey, or overlapped as in the retro-quire at Peterborough. Now it was no longer essential for ribs and infilling to be separate pieces of stone. Instead the fans were built as thin shells with stones of whatever sizes were available; the ribs then became mere projections cut in relief on the surface with recessed panels between, all regardless of the stone joints. As each fan grows from its springing point, one panel branches into two, two into four, and so on. It is hard to realize that this is not a series of stone cones mysteriously defying gravity, but still an arch system bridging the space between wall and wall. The final *tour de force* was the insertion of much bigger stones as pendants at precisely selected points in the arches, as at Oxford (61) and in the incredibly complex roof of Henry VII's Chapel at Westminster Abbey.

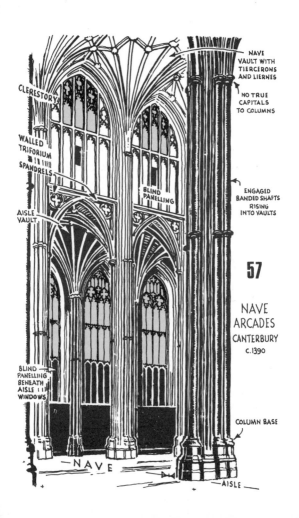

NAVE VAULT WITH TIERCERONS AND LIERNES

NO TRUE CAPITALS TO COLUMNS

CLERESTORY

WALLED TRIFORIUM SPANDRELS

ENGAGED BANDED SHAFTS RISING INTO VAULTS

BLIND PANELLING

AISLE VAULT

57

NAVE ARCADES CANTERBURY c.1390

BLIND PANELLING BENEATH AISLE WINDOWS

COLUMN BASE

NAVE

AISLE

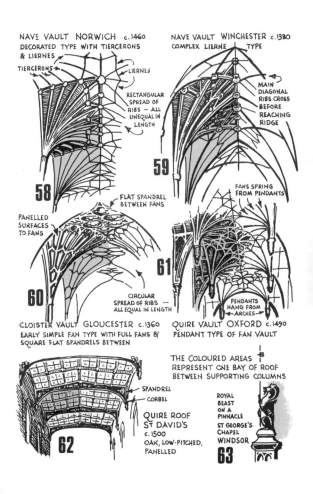

NAVE VAULT NORWICH c.1460
DECORATED TYPE WITH TIERCERONS & LIERNES

TIERCERONS

LIERNES

RECTANGULAR SPREAD OF RIBS — ALL UNEQUAL IN LENGTH

58

NAVE VAULT WINCHESTER c.1380
COMPLEX LIERNE TYPE

MAIN DIAGONAL RIBS CROSS BEFORE REACHING RIDGE

59

PANELLED SURFACES TO FANS

FLAT SPANDREL BETWEEN FANS

60

CIRCULAR SPREAD OF RIBS — ALL EQUAL IN LENGTH

CLOISTER VAULT GLOUCESTER c.1360
EARLY SIMPLE FAN TYPE WITH FULL FANS & SQUARE FLAT SPANDRELS BETWEEN

FANS SPRING FROM PENDANTS

61

PENDANTS HANG FROM ARCHES

QUIRE VAULT OXFORD c.1490
PENDANT TYPE OF FAN VAULT

SPANDREL

CORBEL

QUIRE ROOF
ST DAVID'S
c.1500
OAK, LOW-PITCHED, PANELLED

62

THE COLOURED AREAS REPRESENT ONE BAY OF ROOF BETWEEN SUPPORTING COLUMNS

ROYAL BEAST ON A PINNACLE
ST GEORGE'S CHAPEL WINDSOR

63

The increase in size of windows meant that the thrusts from roof vaults could no longer be spread over the whole length of walls. Looking now at the outside, we therefore find buttresses projecting much further in order to carry these diagonal loads to the ground; flying buttresses, though not a new idea, were more extensively used to bridge the roofs of aisles (64).

Arches were more and more often four-centred, the Tudor arch (65), through the influence of fan-vault shapes and the simplification of tracery.

The triforium practically vanished and become merged with the clerestory in internal design (57). More attention than ever before was paid to the unity of design; for example mouldings that commence near floor level can frequently be followed past the column capitals, upwards through a vestigial triforium and a clerestory, and into the vault. Columns thus have often only partial capitals, terminating perhaps the corner shafts only, and they seldom comprise more than plain mouldings; similar bands or rings sometimes punctuate the shafts at intermediate levels, but much less strongly than in the Early English style. Column bases are generally much taller than hitherto.

The typical window pattern developed into little more than a series of rectangles for the insertion of stained glass figures of saints. The transoms, or horizontal stone bars, were as essential for forming these frames as for ensuring the stability of the tall thin vertical mullions (66, 67). As the traceried heads became increasingly rectilinear, quatrefoils and more fanciful shapes were gradually, though never entirely, abandoned. The treatment of glass was more delicate than before; pinnacled canopies and inscribed scrolls occurred in profusion.

Doorways, too, were often Tudor-arched, the arch usually being enclosed in a square-headed frame with carved spandrels. Important openings were nearly always capped or flanked externally with saint-niches

(*69*). Mouldings now strongly emphasized the linear patterns of the architecture. They have been likened to the earlier shapes turned inside out, to form a series of sharp lines between rounded hollows (*65*).

In contrast with earlier styles there is a marked monotony and indeed poverty of detail. A Perpendicular building never takes so long to examine, for there is so much symmetry and repetition.

Heraldry, usually fully tinctured, provided the basis for much sculpture. Some of the favourite places for detailed carving of this kind were roof bosses and pendants, the ends of the labels or dripstones over windows, and the hollows of string courses at the tops of walls; as before this was largely a labour of devotion. Battlements, their defensive origin set aside, were pierced and fretted and punctuated with pinnacles to produce restless spiky skylines, while heraldic beasts and monsters crowned the buttresses (*63*) and formed gargoyles or water-spouts. Statues of saints in little canopied niches abounded (*68*) and narrative sculpture, such as the well-known Jacob's Ladder on the west front of Bath Abbey, was now virtually confined to religious subjects. The little chantry chapels, like miniature churches in themselves, are precious treasure-houses of these fascinating details; specially good series are to be found at Canterbury, Exeter, Lincoln, Norwich, St Alban's, Wells and, above all, Winchester (*92*).

Before leaving the medieval styles we should glance at timber roofs which, though almost universal in parish churches, are less commonly seen in the great cathedrals; above the vaults, however, a massive frame of timber almost always supports the actual covering of lead or tiles. The earlier roofs are usually the steepest in pitch and the later ones, like those of Manchester, Newcastle and St David's (*62*), are nearly flat with heavy moulded beams, carved wooden bosses and often angel-corbels.

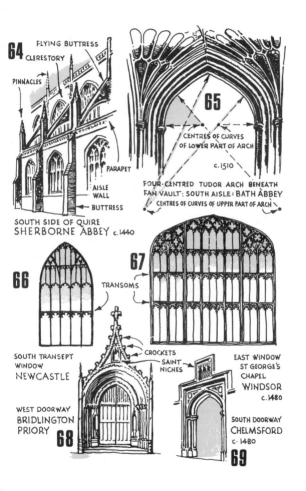

64
FLYING BUTTRESS
CLERESTORY
PINNACLES
PARAPET
AISLE WALL
BUTTRESS

SOUTH SIDE OF QUIRE
SHERBORNE ABBEY c.1440

65
CENTRES OF CURVES
OF LOWER PART OF ARCH
c.1510
CENTRES OF CURVES OF UPPER PART OF ARCH

FOUR-CENTRED TUDOR ARCH BENEATH
FAN VAULT: SOUTH AISLE: BATH ABBEY

66
SOUTH TRANSEPT
WINDOW
NEWCASTLE

TRANSOMS

67
EAST WINDOW
ST GEORGE'S
CHAPEL
WINDSOR
c.1480

WEST DOORWAY
BRIDLINGTON
PRIORY **68**

CROCKETS
SAINT
NICHES

SOUTH DOORWAY
CHELMSFORD
c.1480
69

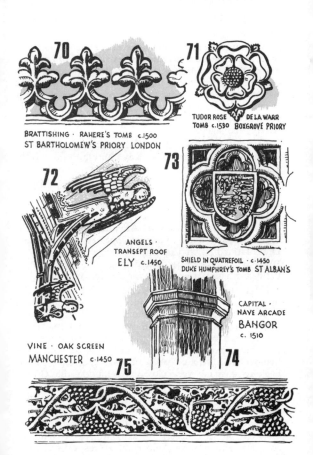

70

BRATTISHING · RAHERE'S TOMB c.1500
ST BARTHOLOMEW'S PRIORY LONDON

71

TUDOR ROSE · DE LA WARR
TOMB c.1530 BOXGROVE PRIORY

72

ANGELS ·
TRANSEPT ROOF
ELY c.1450

73

SHIELD IN QUATREFOIL · c.1450
DUKE HUMPHREY'S TOMB ST ALBAN'S

CAPITAL ·
NAVE ARCADE
BANGOR
c. 1510

VINE · OAK SCREEN
MANCHESTER c.1450 **75**

74

RENAISSANCE, late sixteenth to early nineteenth century

As we have seen in Chapter 1, sweeping changes affected the Church in the sixteenth century. A wave of fanatical destruction wrought havoc in its buildings at the behest of the reformers, to be followed during the Civil War a century later by an even greater outburst in the form of anti-religious mania that left the cathedrals of Carlisle and Lichfield virtually in ruins and all the others irreparably damaged.

At the time of the Reformation of religion ideas of architectural change were already filtering through from Italy. Designers there had never entirely given up their reliance on classical (that is ancient Roman) models, but with the Renaissance or re-birth of learning these were studied much more seriously and gradually provided the only acceptable basic vocabulary of building throughout most of Europe. Architects, as scholars of building history and design, now appeared as individuals. One of the first in England was Inigo Jones, who in 1632-42 began extensive remodelling of the outside of St Paul's Cathedral, London, in the classical style.

After the Great Fire of 1666, which reduced the medieval St. Paul's to a ruin, Sir Christopher Wren undertook its complete rebuilding. This is the only major English cathedral in the classical or Renaissance style. Wren based his first plans on a vast Protestant preaching space (as distinct from the longer forms demanded by Catholic ritual), but was eventually forced back to a shape very closely resembling the Gothic cruciform plan, and to a form of construction that still comprised arcades, clerestory, vaults and concealed flying buttresses (76, 124).

The details and proportions of classical buildings are dictated by the 'orders' – standardized systems of columns with pedestals and entablatures derived from

ancient Roman prototypes. The Doric column (79) has
a plain moulded capital, the Ionic (80) a double spiral
or volute and the Corinthian (78) a bell shape decked
with acanthus leaves. Each of these has its own standard
base and pedestal as well as its architrave, frieze and
cornice forming the entablature (80). In addition there
is a Tuscan order, simpler than the Doric, and a Composite (76), more ornate than the Corinthian. Pilasters
are flattened versions of columns attached to walls (76).

Classical arches are almost always round-headed, but
sometimes segmental; smaller openings are usually flat
and often capped with pediments, like miniature triangular gables with entablature mouldings (77).

Parapets and similar features generally have rows of
balusters alternating with solid blocks of stone.

Ceilings, often elaborately plastered, may be flat,
coved, cylindrical or domed. Roofs were carried up
higher at significant points in a building to form lanterns, turrets or domes. The west towers of St Paul's
(Pl. G), their waywardness contrasting with the nobility
of the great central dome, are amongst the many beautiful steeples that Wren added to London's skyline.

The free carved ornament of the later seventeenth
century, the work of such men as Grinling Gibbons and
Caius Gabriel Cibber, bears comparison with any ever
produced. Favourite motifs were 'swags' and garlands,
scrolls and cartouches, and the ever-recurring *putti* or
baby angels.

The other two important architects of the English
Renaissance whose work we may see in cathedrals are
Thomas Archer at Birmingham (78) and James Gibbs at
Derby (77). Both were designed as galleried preaching
halls for parish use. Much later (1839) the Roman
Catholic pro-Cathedral of Clifton was begun in the
style of the Greek Revival. Nearer our own time is
Sir Edwin Lutyens' majestic crypt at Liverpool (also
R.C.), a masterpiece destined to remain unfinished.

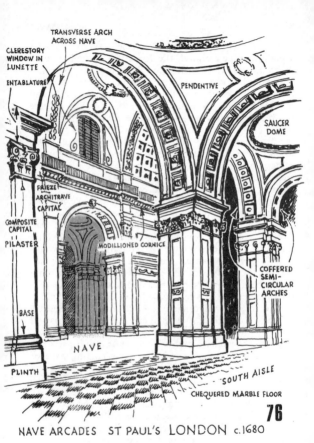

TRANSVERSE ARCH
ACROSS NAVE

CLERESTORY
WINDOW IN
LUNETTE

ENTABLATURE

PENDENTIVE

SAUCER
DOME

FRIEZE
ARCHITRAVE
CAPITAL

COMPOSITE
CAPITAL
PILASTER

MODILLIONED CORNICE

COFFERED
SEMI-
CIRCULAR
ARCHES

BASE

NAVE

PLINTH

SOUTH AISLE

CHEQUERED MARBLE FLOOR

76

NAVE ARCADES ST PAUL'S LONDON c.1680

77

PEDIMENT

FLAT ARCH
KEYSTONE

ARCHITRAVE
ALTERNATING
WITH PLAIN
STONE BLOCKS
(INTERMITTENT
RUSTICATION)

PLINTH

WEST DOORWAY, SOUTH AISLE
DERBY 1723 (GIBBS *Archt.*)

WEATHER VANE

LANTERN

DOME
OR CUPOLA

SCROLLED
BRACKETS

CORNICE

CORINTHIAN
PILASTERS

BELFRY
LOUVRES

78

c.1720 (ARCHER *Archt.*)
TOP OF WEST TOWER BIRMINGHAM

CAPITAL

ROMAN
DORIC
COLUMNS

79

BASE

NORTH ARCADE OF CLOISTER
LINCOLN 1674 (WREN *Archt.*)

CORNICE

FRIEZE

ARCHITRAVE

IONIC CAPITAL

ENTABLATURE

COLUMN

80

CLASSICAL ENTABLATURE ON A MEMORIAL
YORK 1830

VICTORIAN, nineteenth century

In the early years of the nineteenth century there arose an architectural controversy known as the Battle of the Styles, between the Classic Revivalists who held that the only true architecture was that derived from the purest classical sources, and the Gothic School which gained ascendancy from the increasingly scientific opinions of the historians. Pointed architecture soon came to be regarded as the true national style of England and, largely through the influence of the elder Pugin, its revival quickly became a style in itself. To its adherents the renaissance of Gothic was an infinitely worthier cause than the classical revival had ever been.

Pugin, a fervent Roman Catholic, is best known for his collaboration with Barry in the design of the Houses of Parliament. Here, however, we shall be more concerned with the earliest of the Roman Catholic cathedrals built in the years following the Catholic emancipation of 1829. He designed those of Birmingham, Newcastle, Northampton, Nottingham, Shrewsbury and Southwark, though not all were cathedrals from the start and some have later additions by his son and by J. A. Hansom. Not necessarily very English in appearance (Birmingham is a brick building more of North German character), these are usually better buildings outside than in, and often rather wiry in their details.

The next generation, Sir George Gilbert Scott, Butterfield and Street, approached church architecture from what was by then a more soundly based archaeological standpoint, though their buildings – and those of their many contemporaries – are stamped with very personal imprints, Gothic to each being an acquired language within which the artist could exercise his individual skills. Hardly a cathedral in England cannot show some important work by Scott – a partial rebuilding, a new addition, or some splendid fitting in which he interpreted Gothic forms in new materials like cast iron and polished brass. The work of Butterfield, well known for its fanciful decorative patterning in multi-coloured materials and paint, is seen in the Scottish Episcopal cathedrals of Millport and Perth. Street, more solid and historically correct, built the nave of Bristol and added the quire of St Andrew's, Aberdeen.

J. L. Pearson designed Truro Cathedral, and his son the additions to Wakefield. Two other great Victorian architects, Bodley and Burges, are best represented by cathedrals abroad, at Washington and Cork respectively.

The later phases of the Gothic revival (which has lingered on in church building much longer than in other spheres) include the so-called Arts and Crafts Movement of around 1900 (*82*), the work of Sir Giles Gilbert Scott on a monumental scale at Liverpool, Maufe's ingeniously fresh interpretation at Guildford (*84*), Nicholson's rather ungainly work at Portsmouth with its admixture of Italian Romanesque, the freer forms by Bailey and Pace at, for example, Sheffield and Llandaff, and finally the astonishingly traditional current work at Bury St Edmunds by Dykes Bower.

Until quite recently Victorian architecture has been much discredited. Although we may now regret the destruction or well-meant 'improvement' of medieval work, and although it is easy to poke fun at the historical bias, the sentimentalism, and even at the fervent religious convictions and dissensions of the Victorians, the fact is that many cathedrals would have collapsed or been altered out of all recognition if neglect and ignorance had been allowed to continue to take their toll.

ITALIAN
ROMANESQUE
STYLE

81

W·FRONT
CLIFTON (R.C.)
1847 (HANSOM Archt.)

82

'ARTS &
CRAFTS'
GOTHIC
STYLE

TOWER
LEEDS (R.C.)
1902 (EASTWOOD Archt.)

83

S·DOORWAY OF
LADY CHAPEL
LLANDAFF
c.1855 (PRICHARD Archt.)

STONE ARCHES
AND COLUMNS

CROSSING
WITH TOWER
OVER

REINFORCED
CONCRETE
VAULTS
WITH WHITE
PLASTER

LIGHTS
LOUDSPEAKER

ORGAN
CONSOLE
GALLERY

AISLE

BISHOP'S
THRONE

CHOIR   CHOIR

QUIRE & NAVE · GUILDFORD 1936-60

MODERN, twentieth century

To trace the full history of the modern movement in architecture would be impossible and inappropriate in these two pages. Yet the few cathedrals that belong stylistically to the present day are so important that some summary is essential.

The twentieth-century architect's philosophy is one of honesty – honesty in the expression of function and honesty in the expression of construction. He maintains that by following these precepts the true artist cannot help creating beauty. By disregarding them – by, for instance, dressing up a steel-framed building with classical columns and cornices – he would be producing something artificial and characterless, with qualities no more than skin-deep. Gothic architecture was a perfect synthesis of function and construction. The sizes and shapes, the scales and relationships of the parts of any medieval building were determined by the activities that were to take place in it and by the materials and techniques of building available when it was erected. So it should be today.

After nearly four centuries the validity of a backward-looking approach to design began to be questioned (though industrial buildings like warehouses and windmills had long been constructed without inhibitions of style), and towards the end of the nineteenth century the exponents of the Art Nouveau searched for a new style for its own sake. In the 1920s and 1930s progressive architects pushed away the trappings of styles altogether and made a virtue of expressing steel and reinforced concrete frameworks, just as medieval builders had exposed their vaults and buttresses. Since World War II, designers have striven to refine these forms and to give back in terms of modern art something of the ornament and grace that the functionalists had lost.

The architecture of each age can express Christianity

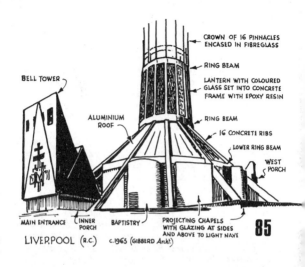

CROWN OF 16 PINNACLES
ENCASED IN FIBREGLASS

RING BEAM

LANTERN WITH COLOURED
GLASS SET INTO CONCRETE
FRAME WITH EPOXY RESIN

RING BEAM

16 CONCRETE RIBS

LOWER RING BEAM

WEST
PORCH

BELL TOWER

ALUMINIUM
ROOF

MAIN ENTRANCE   INNER
PORCH

BAPTISTRY

PROJECTING CHAPELS
WITH GLAZING AT SIDES
AND ABOVE TO LIGHT NAVE

85

LIVERPOOL (R.C.)   c.1965 (GIBBERD Archt.)

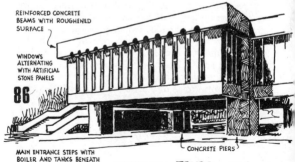

REINFORCED CONCRETE
BEAMS WITH ROUGHENED
SURFACE

WINDOWS
ALTERNATING
WITH ARTIFICIAL
STONE PANELS

86

MAIN ENTRANCE STEPS WITH
BOILER AND TANKS BENEATH

CONCRETE PIERS

CHAPTER HALL TRURO c.1965 (JOHN TAYLOR
Archt.)

equally effectively in its own way; there is no logic in saying that the crown of concrete and fibreglass on Liverpool's new Catholic Cathedral (85) is less spiritually expressive because it is modern than the mock-Gothic tower-top of its Anglican neighbour. Rather is the reverse the case. In recent years most people have come to recognize this and to see that good work of today can live just as happily with its neighbours as Early English does with Norman, or Renaissance with Perpendicular.

Sir Frederick Gibberd's work at Liverpool and Sir Basil Spence's at Coventry (87) are the chief English examples of modern cathedrals, though others are planned. They illustrate the divergent lines of thought confronting church designers today. For Coventry (111) is like a magnified parish church, with what most people regard as a traditional plan-shape: altar at the east end, rather distant, congregation all facing it, and the choir between. Liverpool (165), on the other hand, has a circular plan, with the altar in the centre and the people facing it from all sides. A growing body of priests and people feel that a congregation should be a family gathered around the altar, clearly seeing and participating in ceremonies, and that the sense of mystery and separation imposed by long naves, quires and sanctuaries is inappropriate (hence the nave altar now often introduced into older churches). Many, however, now realize that a completely circular plan is impracticable, for too many see the priest's back and other people's faces, and that the compromise of a semi-circular or similar form is perhaps better.

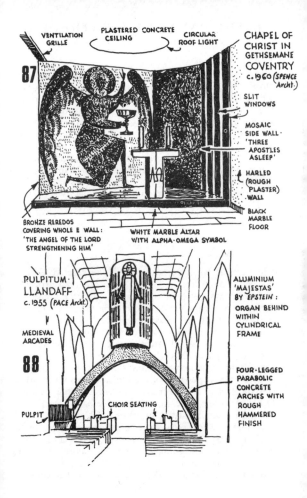

VENTILATION GRILLE

PLASTERED CONCRETE CEILING

CIRCULAR ROOF LIGHT

CHAPEL OF CHRIST IN GETHSEMANE COVENTRY c. 1960 (SPENCE Archt.)

87

SLIT WINDOWS

MOSAIC SIDE WALL · 'THREE APOSTLES ASLEEP'

HARLED (ROUGH PLASTER) WALL

BLACK MARBLE FLOOR

BRONZE REREDOS COVERING WHOLE E WALL: 'THE ANGEL OF THE LORD STRENGTHENING HIM'

WHITE MARBLE ALTAR WITH ALPHA·OMEGA SYMBOL

PULPITUM· LLANDAFF c. 1955 (PACE Archt.)

MEDIEVAL ARCADES

88

PULPIT

CHOIR SEATING

ALUMINIUM 'MAJESTAS' BY EPSTEIN: ORGAN BEHIND WITHIN CYLINDRICAL FRAME

FOUR-LEGGED PARABOLIC CONCRETE ARCHES WITH ROUGH HAMMERED FINISH

3 THE PARTS OF A CATHEDRAL

CLOSES

There is something specially English about the cathedral close, though occasional examples may be found elsewhere (Pisa is an instance). Whereas in other countries the cathedral is almost always hemmed in by noisy streets and other buildings (often erected right against it, regardless of appearance), in England it is set on a green lawn, around which may be found the canons' houses, the choir school, the bishop's palace, and other houses and diocesan buildings. Salisbury has justly the most famous close; out of many others Canterbury, Durham, Exeter, Gloucester, Norwich, Wells and Winchester deserve special mention.

CLOISTERS

Cloisters, as we have seen (p. 12), originated as quiet enclosed courtyards in monasteries, not only providing covered ways between the church, chapter house, refectory, dormitory, etc., but also giving space for meditation and study. Processions would also pass around them, and this is one reason why cathedrals which were never monastic had cloisters nevertheless (Salisbury is a good example); in such cases the walk nearest the cathedral was sometimes omitted, as at Wells (*144*).

The normal position of the cloister is to the south of the south aisle of the nave and west of the transept. Other positions were sometimes necessary according to the nature of the site: Canterbury (*106*), Chester (*109*) and Gloucester (*116*) have northern cloisters while Lérida in Spain (*236*) has a large and very unusual western one. Occasionally there is more than one cloister: Westminster Abbey (*162*) has two and the monastery of Tomar in Portugal no fewer than seven.

89

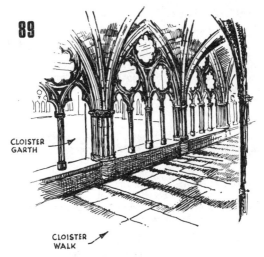

CLOISTER
GARTH

CLOISTER
WALK

Cloister at Bayonne, 13th c.

MONASTIC BUILDINGS

As we have seen (pp. 12–14), not many monasteries
were attached to cathedrals. At the Dissolution most
were abandoned and went to ruin, a process often
accelerated by townspeople who wanted the stone.
Where there are extensive remains, as at Durham (*113*)
and Westminster Abbey (*162*), it is usually because they
were used for storage or for living accommodation as
soon as the monks left. In some cases schools were
established in them (Canterbury) or the prior's house
became the deanery (Norwich, Winchester). Many fine
gatehouses were also preserved, for instance at Bristol
and Norwich, forming effective barriers between the calm
of the close and the bustle of the outside world.

CHAPTER HOUSES

The polygonal meeting-room of the cathedral chapter is one of the most splendid parts of many an English cathedral. Norman chapter houses are square or rectangular (Bristol, *104*), while the Early English and Decorated are often octagonal but sometimes of other shapes; Lincoln, for instance, has ten sides. The planning of circumferential seating (emphasizing the equality of the canons) together with acoustical requirements, the need for dignity and the problems of span and shape presented by the roof, gave designers a special challenge. Indeed, whether or not the central column has been successfully dispensed with (Southwell, for example, *90*), the vault is usually a triumph of craftsmanship in stone. One of the finest of all is that of Wells, which has a central column; this chapter house stands at an upper level beside one of the most graceful flights of steps in the world.

Chapter House, Southwell

Crypt, Worcester

CRYPTS

A crypt enabled the main floor to be raised to a more
commanding level, and was anciently used as a burial-
place. It is, of course, the earliest part of the structure,
and sometimes, at Ripon for instance, it can be very
much older than the building above and quite unrelated
in shape. Occasionally it may extend under the entire
building, like Bourges in France, and form an integral
part of its design. Or it may be under the west end only;
at Le Puy the site slopes so much that the space under
the nave is almost as high as the main columns above.
The crypt beneath the east end of Winchester keeps the

F

floor clear of the flood water rising there every winter.

Some crypts are little more than repositories for rub-bish; some contain beautifully furnished chapels (such as the O.B.E. Chapel in St Paul's, London). At Peel the crypt was a prison (*130*) – like the one near the cloister at Durham (*113*), a reminder of the days when the bishop's authority was not to be regarded lightly. Most crypts are of considerable architectural interest; Gloucester, Worcester (*91*) and York are amongst the best in England, but the finest of all is at Canterbury.

CHANTRY CHAPELS AND MONUMENTS

The most elaborate cathedral memorials are the chan-tries of the fourteenth, fifteenth and early sixteenth centuries, complete miniature chapels set within the main structure, endowed by rich noblemen and clerics so that a priest could pray for their souls for ever. The effigy of the dead person (usually made in his or her lifetime) rests face upwards, often with the hands in a praying position, on a stone tomb-chest decorated with heraldry. Save in exceptional cases, the effigy is of stone, and sometimes it is accompanied by 'weepers' in the form of guardian angels near the head, and by a lion or a dog at the feet. The walls and roof of the chantry are formed of the most intricate stone tracery, ornamented with more heraldry and rich carving of many kinds (*92*).

There are, of course, many other kinds of mem-orials and a listing could start with pre-Conquest carvings like the Hedda Stone at Peterborough. A very full description of the more ordinary kinds can be read in *The Observer's Book of Old English Churches*.

For obvious reasons, cathedrals have always been the resting places of the great; Worcester has the Purbeck marble effigy of King John, *c.* 1230, and the wonderful chantry of Prince Arthur (1504). Edward II's tomb is in the sanctuary at Gloucester. The Black Prince in gilded bronze is at Canterbury (1376); so also is the fan-vaulted chantry of Henry IV. In the crypt of St Paul's is the tomb of Nelson, originally made for Wolsey about 1525.

Two of the most famous English brasses (incised metal plates let into tombstones) are those of Abbot Delamere at St Alban's (*c.* 1360) and Bishop Wyville at Salisbury (1375).

Before leaving the subject of monuments we ought to consider the numerous shrines which, as objects of veneration and pilgrimage, were such an essential part of religious life before the Reformation. Among the most famous were those of St Thomas à Becket at Canterbury and St James at Compostela in Spain. The shrines were in effect monumental tombs, some only large enough to contain a relic of the saint concerned. Usually standing to the east of the high altar, they were jealously guarded, and in one or two cases (e.g. the shrine of St Alban at St Alban's)

Waynflete Chantry, Winchester, c. 1480

the watching chamber has survived. The offerings of pilgrims to such shrines very largely paid for new building operations in the cathedrals and abbeys.

SCREENS AND PULPITUMS

Screens subdivide a church or cathedral, giving privacy to side chapels (*93*) and protection from draughts. If they are of stone or wood, it is generally easy to tell their date from the design of the tracery and mouldings. Exeter has a good series. Wrought iron screens are much rarer; examples from the thirteenth century still survive

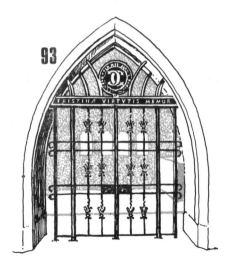

Screen to the Royal Surrey Regimental Chapel, Guildford, c. 1960

(Lincoln east of the crossing) and are generally made up of repeating scroll patterns, but the finest of all are the seventeenth- and eighteenth-century works by Tijou at St Paul's and by Bakewell at Derby.

The screen immediately west of the quire stalls is the pulpitum, and in monastic cathedrals it was supplemented by another screen (called the rood screen because it had a rood or crucifix on it) one bay further west, thus leaving a space between for circulation and processions. Great controversy has often raged (not least in recent years) about the value of the pulpitum or quire screen. According to the opinion of the particular observer, either it punctuates the length of a cathedral, enhancing the sense of space and mystery, or it divides it uncompromisingly into quite separate component parts, and ruins its unity. Many stone pulpitums have been removed and replaced either by 19th-century metalwork or by nothing at all. One, at Chichester, has actually been re-installed after languishing elsewhere for over a century. In some cases, as at Salisbury, the nineteenth-century screen has in its turn been removed in the cause of unity. Yet these screens are nothing compared with the *coro* which, to English eyes, intrudes into the interior of many Spanish cathedrals (*229*).

To mention a few of the pulpitums that remain, Exeter's and Southwell's are sumptuous work of the fourteenth century, while Ripon's is a massive wall partly intended to strengthen the tower. Amongst Welsh cathedrals, the one at St David's is thirteenth century, while at Llandaff the four-legged concrete arch which straddles the quire entrance (*88*) is a daring innovation of the present century; it was designed to carry the organ, a purpose which many older pulpitums have served since the eighteenth century (Pl. E).

Screens and gates across the aisles controlled admission to eastern parts of a cathedral during the canons' services, or to saints' shrines.

SEATING

There are three principal kinds of seating in a cathedral: the bishop's, the choir's and canons', and the congregational. Congregational seating was formerly limited to a few stone seats around the walls, and nowadays the standard kind of seat is the chair, which can fairly easily be cleared away when not wanted. The internal proportions of almost any medieval church are improved if the seats are removed; Ely, the floor of which is usually clear, demonstrates this.

At the other extreme, the bishop's throne (*84, 94*) has always been an object of pride and skill. Two of the finest are at Exeter (1313-17) and St David's. Hexham still possesses its throne of *c.* 680, and the eighth-century seat at Norwich which came from North Elmham has lately been re-installed in the traditional position east of the high altar. Canterbury has the very ancient chair of St Augustine on which every archbishop is enthroned. The eastern position for bishops' thrones was given up in the thirteenth century, when the now-accepted position on the south side of the quire was adopted in England.

In almost every cathedral the quire seating (*246*) is of the greatest aesthetic and historical interest. Usually there are

Bishop's throne, Bordeaux

two rows each side facing inwards. The back row is for the canons and the front for the choir itself. One or both rows are 'returned' at right angles down the east side of the pulpitum, facing the altar, and the seat on the south side nearest the actual doorway in the pulpitum is that of the dean or provost. Medieval canons' stalls usually have arm-rests, and tip-up wooden seats called misereres or misericords (*95*) – derived from the Latin word for pity (*misericordia*) because a ledge was provided on the underside out of compassion for the older clergy who would otherwise have had to stand for long periods during services. Beneath these ledges the wood-carvers would indulge in all sorts of fancies, often depicting animals and rustic scenes. Above the stalls

95

HINGED
SEAT UP –
SHOWING
LEDGE FOR
RESTING
& CARVED
ORNAMENT
BENEATH

SEAT DOWN –
FOR NORMAL
SITTING

*Quire stalls with
misericords, Blackburn*

are elaborate canopies – richly pinnacled and traceried hoods which frequently bear the titles of the prebendaries who use them. Some of the finest quire stalls in England are those of the fourteenth century at Chester, Ely, Exeter, Hereford and Lincoln.

ORGANS

The use of the organ in cathedrals and churches for the accompaniment of plainsong began at least as early as the twelfth century, its development into the 'king of instruments' that we know today having been a gradual process. Many of the finest organs are in Germany, where music and musical instruments were brought to near-perfection in the eighteenth century; the largest of all is at Passau. In the nineteenth century they tended to become over-large, but lately there has been a welcome tendency not only to return to the purity of the smaller organs but also to revive the use of little chamber organs such as the one at Salisbury.

Usually the organ-case is one of the most splendid examples of the wood-carver's art in a cathedral. Amongst very many in England, those of Bristol (1682-85), St Paul's (begun 1694) and, on a smaller scale, Wakefield, are specially notable. Sometimes the organ is arranged on one or both sides of the quire, as in St Paul's; sometimes, as at Exeter (Pl. E), the medieval pulpitum has been used as the support for a grand display of pipework, interrupting but adding splendour to the long sweeping vista of the interior. At Llandaff the modern four-legged parabolic arch (88) also holds part of the organ; this sort of arrangement, with the playing console at floor level, is now made possible electrically.

BELLS

One of the principal purposes of a cathedral tower is the hanging of bells. For their origin we would have to look even further back into history than for organs; the early round towers of Ireland, for instance, were probably bell-towers or, to use the Italian word, *campanili*. Bells were intended as indications of the times of mass or service, for summoning the devoted, for tolling at funerals and for pealing on joyful occasions. Ringing for the beauty of their sound, or for the satisfaction of the physical and mental exertion, came later.

In English belfries with eight or even twelve or more bells, change-ringing is widely practised. This consists in the ringing, in succession, of a series of permutations in the sequence of the bells, mathematically worked out so as to avoid abrupt changes in rhythm for any one ringer. The number of different sequences of only seven bells (if the eighth is 'fixed' in each run) is 5,040; a correct peal is thus no mean feat, and cathedral towers often contain records of past achievements proudly painted on boards. During a peal the large, finely balanced wheels on which the bells are mounted turn over in a complete revolution. When the bells are sounded by the hammers of the clock mechanism, however, they remain at rest, hanging downwards.

On the Continent, in the Low Countries in particular, carillons are not uncommon. Their essential component is a revolving drum into which metal pegs are set to trigger the bell-hammers. The drum is coupled to the clock, and can be pre-set to play tunes instead of ordinary chimes. English examples can be found at Selby Abbey and Derby.

CLOCKS

Clocks have always been fascinating to their makers and users. The primitive clock is the sundial of which thousands still remain on churches, with or without their gnomons or shafts, marked with the times of masses or services.

There is no essential difference between a cathedral clock and any other large one, except that greater skills were lavished on them and greater care has sometimes been taken in their preservation. The most famous are the astronomical clocks which indicate the phases of the moon and similar information, some of which seems quaint to modern eyes (*96*). Sometimes puppet-like figures appear at each hour and perform a series of antics before going behind the scenes again. Examples are at Wells (*c.* 1390) and at Beauvais in France.

Clock in N transept at Exeter c. 1480 (upper dial c. 1760)

LIBRARIES

In their day the medieval monasteries were virtually the only centres of learning. They thus amassed a wealth of manuscript literature, by no means all of it religious in character. Although most was destroyed and dispersed at the Reformation, some cathedral chapters managed to retain a small proportion of their treasures and added to them in succeeding centuries. Such was the value of books even then that they were chained to the desks, and one of the most famous chained collections is to be found over the north transept at Hereford, also the fortunate possessor of a *Mappa Mundi* or world map of *c.* 1280. The cathedral libraries of Winchester and St Paul's are justly noted as well.

GLASS

The subject of cathedral glass is a vast one. Whole books could be, and have been, written about the windows of individual cathedrals, and what follows can only be a superficial survey.

In the Romanesque period glass was a luxury which few could afford. It was restricted to small panes separately coloured and leaded together with strips called cames. In their simplest form the iron bars holding the whole window flat in its stone surround are called saddle-bars; where, later, they were formed into patterns in their own right, they are sometimes known as *ferramenta*.

Methods of colouring improved throughout the Middle Ages. Twelfth- and thirteenth-century glass is comparatively crude in its delineation of forms and has a predominance of reds and blues, as at Canterbury and Chartres. Late thirteenth-century glass is greyish (grisaille) as in the Five Sisters at York. By the fifteenth century much more subtle methods of drawing had been perfected, and the colour range extended to include endless and beautiful variations of golden yellows, browns and greens. The intensity of colour depends on the thickness of the glass as well as skilled control of the stains introduced whilst it is molten. Several English cathedrals have foreign glass, such as the Flemish in Lichfield's Lady Chapel.

Some of the ancient techniques were recaptured in the nineteenth century, but Victorian glass can be distinguished without difficulty by its new appearance, by the naiveté of the subject-matter, or by its rather characterless figure-drawing. Glass of the seventeenth and eighteenth centuries is occasionally met with, and can be identified by its large areas of raw colour, with the panes generally rectangular instead of following the patterns of the subject.

In the present century many methods of manufacture and design have been tried, a lot of them frankly experimental. The most typical, as in the great new windows of Coventry, rejects nearly all the pictorial refinements and subtleties of Gothic and reverts to brilliant interplays of colours and abstract patterns.

WALL-PAINTINGS and TAPESTRIES

Wall-paintings complemented glass in the medieval church by providing a series of illustrated stories which all could understand. Very few remain today, though Canterbury has an unequalled twelfth-century series in the crypt. Very few, especially, have endured the English climate, and many that do exist owe their survival to the Puritans who buried them under whitewash. Rediscovered in the course of the last century or so, they have proved almost impossible to preserve satisfactorily. Roofs, arches and most other surfaces were painted, with a splendour hard to imagine now that only unintelligible patches of pigment remain in nearly every instance. Where full colouring and gilding have been restored according to historical evidence, the result appears to our eyes to be much too rich and gaudy.

Tapestries hardly exist in English cathedrals, with the exception of the great seated figure of Christ at Coventry, commissioned when the cathedral was rebuilt after the Second World War. On the Continent, however, there are many magnificent examples as at Soissons and Aix-en-Provence.

SANCTUARY FITTINGS

Failing a great east window, the most splendid treatment of the wall behind the altar was a carved reredos, with tier upon tier of saints in canopied niches. Few survived the reformers' zeal: one of the best is the mid-fourteenth century example at Christchurch Priory.

The high altar is often crowned by a *baldacchino* or canopy on columns; where it stands well clear of the east wall there may alternatively be a hanging 'tester'. The altar itself is of stone or wood and carries two or six candlesticks. There is also a Cross or Crucifix, unless one hangs above or is prominently incorporated into the wall or window pattern behind.

The altar frontals, changing in colour with the Church seasons, are usually magnificent pieces of embroidered fabric; the few ancient examples that exist are, of course, too delicate for everyday use. With frontals, vestments and soft furnishings in a modern idiom Chichester Cathedral has in late years revived the ancient patronage of art by the Church.

The small shelf or table near the altar is the credence and is used by the priest for holy vessels at times of communion. The piscina (the bowl for disposal of holy water) and sedilia (seats for the clergy celebrating mass) are often fine examples of medieval carvers' art.

97

Font, Hereford

Rochester has particularly good stone sedilia of the fourteenth century, while at St David's, a century later, they are made of oak.

The communion rail, before which the people kneel or stand to receive the consecrated bread and wine, is of metal, wood or sometimes stone. In most English cathedrals it has been renewed in the nineteenth century, but Derby has a superb eighteenth-century example in wrought iron.

PULPITS

Many cathedrals have more than one pulpit, not only because an older one has not been altogether discarded when a new one has been installed, but also because they are needed in side chapels for smaller congregations. A wide variety of styles and materials may be found. In the nave of Wells there is one of stone, *c.* 1530, unusual not only for its pre-Reformation origin but also for the early Renaissance detail. Carlisle has a carved wooden pulpit of 1559 which came from a church in Antwerp. Contrasting ones of very recent design are at St Paul's (classical, with wood-carving matching the Grinling Gibbons work) and Chichester (cast aluminium with 'primitive' abstract patterns).

LECTERNS

A number of pre-Reformation lecterns exist in England, mostly of brass in the form of eagles with outstretched wings. Exeter and Southwell possess them, while Norwich has a pelican. At Canterbury the eagle dates from 1663, a time when many church fittings had to be renewed after the ravages of the Civil War.

FONTS

Because they are often no bigger than parish church fonts, those in cathedrals are often overlooked, but they are usually of very real interest, and a wide variety of styles and dates exists (*97*). Chichester's and Winchester's are both Norman with Biblical scenes, the one of Purbeck marble and the other of black marble from Tournai in Belgium. Chester's is of black marble, too, but in Renaissance style. Durham's, though dated 1663, has Gothic as well as classical features in its sumptuous wooden cover. Bradford possesses a fine pinnacled cover of the fifteenth century. At Norwich the bowl is embellished with sculptures of the Seven Sacraments, a popular theme throughout East Anglia. St Paul's, not surprisingly, has a splendid and very large elliptical marble font in keeping with the building. At Truro red porphyry, one of the stones so loved by the Victorians, is used, and at Coventry a rough boulder from the Holy Land.

LIGHTING

Electric lighting is nowadays used so universally as an aid to finding one's way about, to reading books and music, and to appreciating architecture either by gentle

illumination or by means of dramatic displays such as *Son et Lumière*, that the older forms – gas, candles, rush lights – are very hard to imagine in the same settings.

Much ingenuity has been used in designing and positioning ordinary lamps and spot lights and flood lights, and even sometimes in combining lights and loudspeakers in single hanging fittings as in Guildford (*84*). Of the older forms that survive, the many-branched candelabra of the seventeenth and eighteenth centuries, usually of polished brass, are by far the most gracious (*98*).

Brass candelabrum,
Southwark, 1680

4 CATHEDRALS OF ENGLAND AND WALES

PLANS OF CATHEDRALS

The plans in this book are all to the scale of 1 : 2,500, shown below. They are simplified to bring out the main features; for more accurate details it is essential to consult bigger drawings. For example, all walls are drawn as though they were of the same thickness and all columns as though they were of the same size. Towers are indicated with a T and their supporting piers drawn rather larger than ordinary columns. Doorways, windows and buttresses are omitted, but the quire stalls and altar are shown diagrammatically. What is called the east end of a church (i.e. the altar end) usually does face east; north is thus usually at the top of the page.

The colouring on each wall indicates its period according to the key on p. 16, and the colouring *between* walls the date of the roof (or steeple) above. Brecon, as an example (p. 84), has mostly Early English walls (coloured orange) but Victorian roofs (grey). Frequently walls are of three different periods – the base the oldest, the upper part rebuilt later, the windows inserted last of all – and a single plan cannot possibly give so much information. The principle here is to give precedence to the earliest work, thus showing how a building has evolved but not necessarily coinciding with our first impression on seeing it. Tinted walls with white areas between usually indicate ruins.

From Chapter 7 (p. 133) onwards the plans are in black and white only, because the dated periods of English architecture do not apply outside this country.

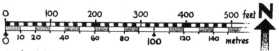

Scale 1 : 2500

APPROXIMATE NORTH FOR ALL PLANS

99

BANGOR

100

 BIRMINGHAM

101

BLACKBURN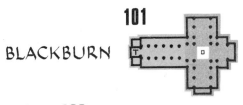

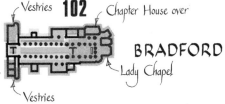

Vestries **102** Chapter House over

BRADFORD

Lady Chapel

Vestries

BANGOR St Deiniol
Diocese: Anglesey, Caernarvonshire, W Merionethshire, W Montgomeryshire

Diocese founded 546. Successively rebuilt. Destroyed by Owen Glendower 1402. Tower and nave rebuilt 1496-1532 (*74*). E end, transepts and base of crossing-tower 1868 (Scott).

BIRMINGHAM St Philip
Diocese: NW Warwickshire

Parish church of 1711-25, created a cathedral 1905.

Classical, by Thomas Archer, designed as preaching-hall with galleries. Square fluted piers carrying semi-circular arches; flat ceiling. Graceful lantern-tower (*78*).

Elaborate iron screen in Tijou's style. Excellent late 19th-c. glass by Burne-Jones.

BLACKBURN St Mary   Diocese: N Lancashire

Parish church rebuilt 1820-26, made a cathedral 1926. E end with transepts then added by Forsythe. Crossing-lantern and spire over centralized altar 1961, by Laurence King.

BRADFORD St Peter
Diocese: extreme W Yorkshire

Parish church, a cathedral since 1919.

Low embattled 15th c.; arcades earlier. S side rebuilt 1832-3. Transepts 1899. Enlarged E end and western additions by Maufe *c.* 1950-60.

Fine Morris glass in chancel. Richly pinnacled 15th-c. font cover.

BRECON   St John the Evangelist
          Diocese (Swansea and Brecon): Brecknockshire,
                    Radnorshire and extreme W Glamorgan

Benedictine priory church, parochial since Reformation
and a cathedral since 1923.

Mostly 13th c. (*35*), plain, grey and tree-girt. Unique
30-cupped cresset stone. 12th-c. font.

Remaining priory buildings restored to cathedral use.

BRISTOL   Holy Trinity
          Diocese: extreme S Gloucestershire and N Wiltshire

Augustinian abbey founded 1140. Served as cathedral
(mainly for the county of Dorset!) 1542-1836. Status
restored 1897 after completion.

Rich Norman chapter house (*10*). Broad 14th-c. quire
and aisles of hall-church design (equal in height) with
inventive, if capricious, detail: aisles have transverse
arches as internal flying buttresses, carrying little rib-
vaults (*44*). Nave and W towers by Street, begun 1868.

Stalls with misericords *c.* 1520. 15th-c. brass candelabrum in Berkeley Chapel. Late Saxon carving of
Harrowing of Hell in S transept. Many monuments,
including several to abbots. Organ cases 1682-5.

Extensive abbey remains intermingled with later
buildings include Great Gatehouse and E walk of
cloister.

BURY ST EDMUNDS   St James
          Diocese (St Edmundsbury and Ipswich): Suffolk

Former parish church, rebuilt early in 16th c. under
shadow of one of the greatest Benedictine abbeys. Detached 12th-c. bell-tower. 19th-c. chancel now demolished and newly replaced by quire and aisles.
Transepts and central tower by Dykes Bower, still in
modern Gothic style.

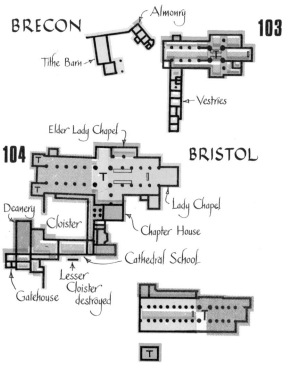

BRECON

Almonry

Tithe Barn

103

Vestries

104

Elder Lady Chapel

BRISTOL

T

T

T

Lady Chapel

Deanery

Cloister

Chapter House

Cathedral School

Gatehouse

Lesser
Cloister
destroyed

T

BURY ST EDMUNDS **105**

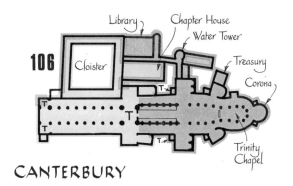

CANTERBURY

Library · Chapter House · Water Tower · Treasury · Corona · Cloister · Trinity Chapel

106

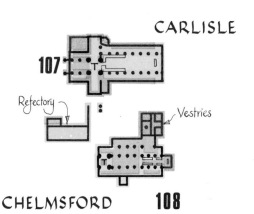

CARLISLE

107

Refectory · Vestries

CHELMSFORD   108

CANTERBURY Christ
Diocese: E Kent and extreme NE Surrey

Splendid cathedral of Archbishops and pilgrims, possibly founded before St Augustine (602).

Three main architectural phases: Norman, the quire walls, with double-apsed transepts and pretty miniature towers; very early Gothic (French in character), the quire interior (*24, 26*) (constricted by keeping two Norman chapels), retro-quire and corona; Perpendicular, the stately nave (*57*), cloister and magnificent 'Bell Harry' tower. Extensive crypts: the western Norman with unsurpassed carved capitals (*12*), the eastern spacious Early English.

Glowing 12th- and 13th-c. glass. 17th-c. stallwork. 14th- and 15th-c. screens. 'St Augustine's Chair' in corona. Henry IV's Chantry and Black Prince's bronze effigy flanking site of Becket's shrine.

Priory buildings (partly 12th c.) incorporated in King's School.

CARLISLE Holy Trinity
Diocese: Cumberland and Westmorland

Augustinian monastery founded 1102, diocese 1133.

Two bays only of 12th-c. nave; remaining six destroyed by Scots about 1650. Fine quire and aisles 14th c., with grand curvilinear E window (*48*).

Pulpit of 1559 from Antwerp. Early 15th-c. canopied stalls. Interesting screens.

Remains of cloister and chapter house. Refectory now the cathedral library. Gatehouse of 1527.

CHELMSFORD St Mary, St Peter and St Cedd
Diocese: Essex

Parish church, made a cathedral 1914.

Largely 15th c. Nave 1801-3. Outer N aisle 1873. New E end by Nicholson, 1926-9. Flint flushwork porch (*69*). Steeple 1749.

CHESTER   Christ and St Mary   Diocese: Cheshire

Benedictine abbey founded 1093. Created a cathedral 1541.

Unusual plan cramped by city wall, hence N transept still primitive Norman but S transept extended on grand scale in 14th c. Lady Chapel 13th c.; progressive rebuilding of quire and nave from E to W; W front early Tudor. Severe nave without triforium. Vaults almost all 19th c., but on the whole more distinguished inside than out. Red sandstone walls heavily restored.

Superb quire stalls rich with pinnacles and delicate carving; 48 splendid misericords. Renaissance black marble font.

Chapter house, early 13th c., architecturally the best part. Cloister 15th c.; considerable remains of adjoining 12th-c. abbot's house and refectory.

CHICHESTER   Holy Trinity   Diocese: Sussex

See transferred from Selsey c. 1080.

Informal cathedral of modest size and complex history. Basically 12th c. Nave and W part of quire remodelled and vaulted after severe fire 1187; retro-quire beautiful very early Gothic. Unusual outer nave chapels Geometric Decorated, also clumsy enlargement of Lady Chapel. Central steeple rebuilt 1861-66 after telescopic collapse, and NW tower 1901. Detached bell-tower 15th c.

Arundel screen (pulpitum) c. 1470; two important Romanesque panels of figure carving from previous screen, c. 1140. Quire stalls c. 1330, not of first quality. Poor 19th-c. glass. Aluminium pulpit 1966 and other recent furnishings.

Unusual cloister surrounding S transept, c. 1400, largely of timber. Many delightful houses adjoining it.

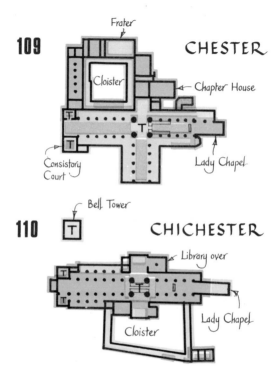

109

Frater

CHESTER

Cloister

Chapter House

T

Consistory
Court

Lady Chapel

Bell Tower

110 T

CHICHESTER

Library over

T
T

Lady Chapel

Cloister

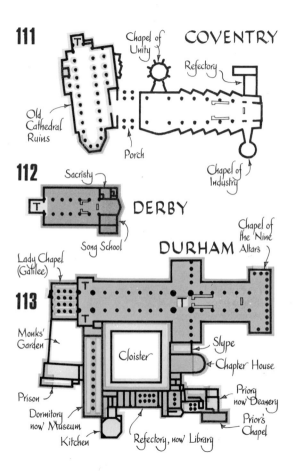

111   COVENTRY

Chapel of Unity

Refectory

Old Cathedral Ruins

Porch

Chapel of Industry

112   Sacristy

DERBY

Song School

DURHAM

Chapel of the Nine Altars

Lady Chapel (Galilee)

113

Monks' Garden

Slype

Cloister

Chapter House

Prison

Priory now Deanery

Dormitory now Museum

Prior's Chapel

Kitchen

Refectory, now Library

COVENTRY   St Michael

Diocese: Warwickshire except NW

Former priory, now with scanty remains, was seat of bishop 1095-1129. Parish church of St Michael, 1373 to c. 1450, created a cathedral 1918.

Gutted by fire bombs 1940 and retained as roofless ruin; 295-foot steeple intact. Adjacent new cathedral by Spence consecrated 1962.

Green tapestry of seated Christ by Sutherland, dominating interior. Innumerable works in glass, metal, stone and wood representing the best of mid-20th-c. applied arts (87).

DERBY   All Saints   Diocese: Derbyshire

Parish and former collegiate church, created a cathedral 1927.

Tower c. 1500. Remainder classical, mainly by Gibbs, 1723-5 (77), but E end by Sebastian Comper c. 1965. Intricate 18th-c. screens and other ironwork. Bishop's throne supposedly 18th-c. Turkish.

DURHAM   Christ and St Mary

Diocese: County Durham

Settled by monks 999 and refounded around St Cuthbert's shrine 1081 as fortified Benedictine cathedral-monastery on dominating rock above River Wear.

Supreme masterpiece of Romanesque architecture, 1093-1135. Overwhelmingly solemn alternation of round and clustered columns. Exceptionally early large-scale vaulting. Lighter Galilee Lady Chapel 1170-5 (15), rich with zigzag. Eastern Chapel of Nine Altars 1242-c. 1285. Central tower heightened in 15th c.

Splendid 17th-c. wood carving in screens, stalls and font cover. Famous 12th-c. knocker. Bishop's throne over Hatfield chantry, 1381. Reredos 1372-80.

Cloister buildings basically Norman. Later monks' dormitory (now museum) and uniquely vaulted kitchen.

ELY   Holy Trinity
            Diocese: Cambridgeshire, Huntingdonshire and
                                              extreme W Norfolk

Monastery founded 673. Present building begun 1083; became a cathedral 1109.

Norman nave with main transept and W transept and huge turreted and arcaded W tower (*17*). Extreme E end rebuilt 1234-52 (*27*). Crossing majestically reconstructed in octagonal lanterned form after collapse of central tower in 1322 and subsequent complete removal of its piers; W end of quire also rebuilt after the catastrophe. N arm of W transept fell in 15th c. Lady Chapel in unusual northerly position, completed 1353.

Quire stalls *c.* 1330-40, almost all with original miserere seats; spoilt by heavy Belgian carvings added into upper canopies. Uncommonly extensive display of 19th-c. glass. Many bishops' monuments, including Alcock and West chantries, 1501 and 1534, each side of E end.

Cloister mostly gone. Gatehouse ('Ely Porta') 1397. Remains of other monastic buildings in old Bishops' Palace, King's School and elsewhere.

EXETER   St Peter   Diocese: Devon

Diocese transferred from Crediton 1050.

Plain Norman towers unusually placed over transepts. Remainder rebuilt from E end westwards 1275 to *c.* 1370 (Pl. E). Very homogeneous in character with profusely clustered columns and rich vaults (*40*). So-called Minstrels' Gallery, level with N nave triforium.

14th-c. stone pulpitum and several other fine screens. Elaborate sedilia in quire. Bishop's throne 1313-17, extravagantly pinnacled. 13th-c. misericords in 19th-c. quire stalls. 15th-c. brass eagle lectern. Clock of 1376 and 1760. Many monuments to bishops.

Rectangular chapter house 13th c. (with later vault); cloister virtually disappeared.

ELY

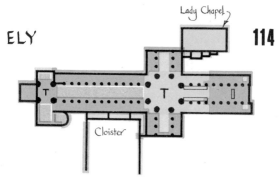

Lady Chapel

114

T

T

Cloister

EXETER

115

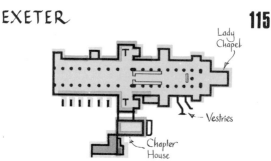

Lady Chapel

T

T

Vestries

Chapter House

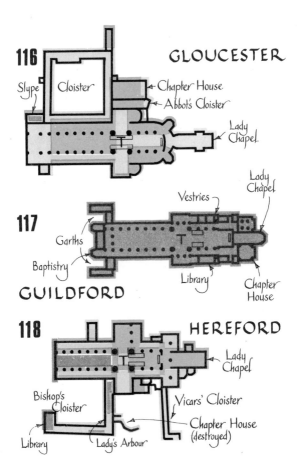

116 GLOUCESTER

Slype

Cloister

Chapter House

Abbot's Cloister

Lady Chapel

117

Vestries

Lady Chapel

Garths

Baptistry

Library

Chapter House

GUILDFORD

118 HEREFORD

Lady Chapel

Bishop's Cloister

Vicars' Cloister

Library

Lady's Arbour

Chapter House (destroyed)

GLOUCESTER Holy Trinity
Diocese: Gloucestershire, except extreme S

St Peter's monastery founded 681; church became cathedral 1541.

Basically Norman (1089-1160), with extensive crypt. Nave with massive piers (*6*); low vault added *c.* 1240 and W end rebuilt *c.* 1430. Quire and transepts remodelled *c.* 1340 with delicate tracery embroidered over earlier stonework, and high complex vault extending beneath tower (the earliest instance of the Perpendicular style (Pl. F)). Vast E window honouring fallen at Crécy. Central tower and Lady Chapel *c.* 1460.

Rich mid-14th-c. quire stalls. Pinnacled tomb of Edward II, 1327. Abbots' and bishops' monuments.

Fan-vaulted cloister (*60*) 1381-1412, complete with study carrels and lavatorium; 12th-c. chapter house.

GUILDFORD Holy Spirit   Diocese: W Surrey

Diocese founded 1927. Entirely new cathedral by Maufe 1936-65, on commanding hill-site. Simplified Gothic: red brick outside, stone and plaster within (*84*).

HEREFORD St Mary & St Ethelbert
Diocese: Herefordshire and S Shropshire

Diocese founded late in 7th c.

Exceptionally complex building sequence. Basically early 12th c. in arcades and crossing. N transept *c.* 1250, inspired by Westminster Abbey. Retro-quire and rich Lady Chapel slightly earlier. Tower and E transepts 14th c. Nave shortened *c.* 1790 and upper parts rebuilt. W front 1902-8 (Oldrid Scott).

Early 14th-c. quire stalls. *Mappa Mundi c.* 1280. Delicately canopied monument to Bishop Aquablanca, 1268.

Cloister mostly 15th c.   College of Vicars Choral to SE, 15th c.   Bishop's Palace to SW, built around 12th-c. hall.

LEICESTER   St Martin   Diocese: Leicestershire

Parish church, made a cathedral 1927.

Mostly 19th c. outside: over-high central steeple by Brandon, dignified S porch by Bodley. Interior largely 13th and 14th c., refurnished under Nicholson.

LICHFIELD   St Mary
                          Diocese: Staffordshire and N Shropshire

First church consecrated 700. Diocese long associated with Coventry and Chester.

Mostly c. 1195 (quire and transepts) and c. 1250-1310 (*47*). Severely damaged in Civil War and unsympathetically reconstructed in 19th c. Three spires. Geometric Lady Chapel with 16th-c. Flemish glass.

Bishop's Palace 1687. Half-timbered Vicars' Close.

LINCOLN   St Mary   Diocese: Lincolnshire

See moved from Dorchester (Oxfordshire) 1072. Commanding situation on limestone ridge.

Norman W front (*16*) embedded in great 13th-c. arcaded screen. Nave, double transepts, and St Hugh's quire between them, splendidly rebuilt 1192-1250 after earthquake: mature Early English with much Purbeck marble (*21*, Pl. C); unique asymmetrical quire vault. Angel Quire 1256-80, developing Westminster's Geometric style (*46*) with luxurious 'transparent' double arcading and profuse carving. Superb added doorways into quire aisles from transepts. Grand towers 14th and 15th c.

Early 13th-c. glass collected into transepts and E windows of quire aisles. Outstanding quire stalls c. 1365-70. Glorious 14th-c. pulpitum (*55*). Chantry chapels.

Great decagonal chapter house early 13th c. (*36*). Cloister 14th c., but N walk and library by Wren, 1674 (*79*). 14th-c. Exchequer Gate and precinct walls.

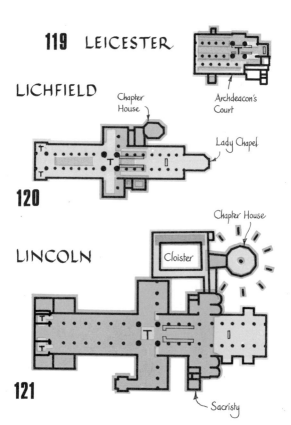

119 LEICESTER

Archdeacon's Court

LICHFIELD

Chapter House

Lady Chapel

120

LINCOLN

Chapter House

Cloister

121

Sacristy

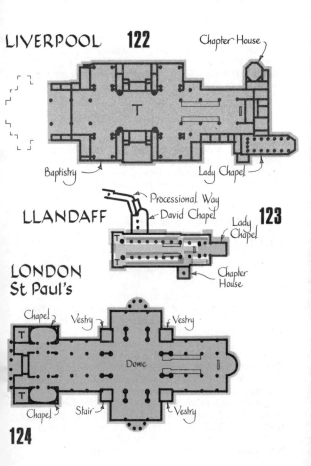

LIVERPOOL **122**

Chapter House

T

Baptistry

Lady Chapel

LLANDAFF **123**

Processional Way

David Chapel

Lady Chapel

T

Chapter House

LONDON
St Paul's

Chapel

Vestry

Vestry

T

Dome

T

Chapel

Stair

Vestry

124

H

LIVERPOOL   Christ

Diocese: SW Lancashire

Diocese founded 1880. Red sandstone cathedral begun 1904 will be surpassed in size only by St Peter's at Rome when complete. Sir Giles Gilbert Scott's interpretation of Gothic on an overwhelming scale.

LLANDAFF   St Peter & St Paul

Diocese: Glamorgan except extreme W

Church reputedly founded 560 by St Teilo.

Present building begun 1130 (*11*); rich Norman arch behind altar. Lady Chapel and nave arches 13th c.   NW tower 15th c. Extensive 19th-c. rebuilding after falling to ruin (*83*); NW tower by Prichard. Shattered by landmine 1941 and restored by Pace; Welch Regiment Chapel added, also parabolic-arched pulpitum bearing organ and Epstein's 'Majestas' (*88*).

LONDON   St Paul

Diocese: City of London and original county of Middlesex

Probably founded 604.

Medieval cathedral mostly 12th and 13th c., seriously damaged in Great Fire 1666, and rebuilt by Wren 1675-1710. The only great English cathedral in Renaissance style (*76*).

Long Gothic-type plan with renowned central lantern-dome 364 feet high. Elegant twin towers (Pl. G) flanking W portico. Two-storey outer screen wall concealing nave clerestory and flying buttresses. Beautiful external sculptured details. Extensive crypt.

Quire stalls by Grinling Gibbons (*246*). Superb carved organ cases. Exquisite wrought iron screens and balustrades by Tijou. In the crypt Nelson's tomb made *c.* 1525 for Wolsey, and Wellington's funeral carriage 1852. Very many later memorials above and below.

MANCHESTER   St Mary, St George & St Denys
                        Diocese: SE Lancashire

Parish church, made collegiate 1421, and a cathedral
1847. Mostly *c.* 1450-70; outer chapels slightly later.
Tower practically rebuilt 1862-8.
   Superb stalls and misericords 1505-10.

NEWCASTLE   St Nicholas
                        Diocese: Northumberland

Parish church, made a cathedral 1882.
   Mostly 14th and 15th c. (*66*). Tower crowned by
daring steeple on flying arches, *c.* 1450. Library 1736.

NEWPORT   St Woolos
                        Diocese (Monmouth): Monmouthshire

Parish church of uncertain antiquity, made a cathedral
1921. W 'galilee' probably represents the pre-Norman
church. 12th-c. nave to east (*13*), reached through rich
semi-circular arch. Plain tower and aisles 15th c.   E end
by Alban Caroe, *c.* 1960.

NORWICH   Holy Trinity
                        Diocese: Norfolk except extreme W

Monastic (Benedictine). See moved from Thetford 1094.
   Mostly 1096-1145 (*9*). Norman interior enhanced by
much later quire clerestory and by lierne vaults
throughout (*58*). Profusion of roof bosses. Unusually
complete chevet (Pl. B). E chapel by Nicholson 1930-2.
315-foot spire *c.* 1480. 14th-c. Prior's Doorway (*51*).
   Bishop's throne in apse. 'Seven Sacraments' font.
Stalls *c.* 1420-80. 15th-c. brass pelican lectern. Goldwell
chantry of 1499 and other bishops' monuments.
   Two-storeyed cloister 1297-1430. Infirmary and refectory ruins. Gateways into close: St Ethelbert's 1316,
Erpingham 1420, Bishop's *c.* 1435, Water Gate 15th c.

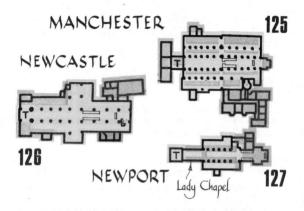

MANCHESTER

125

NEWCASTLE

T

126

NEWPORT   Lady Chapel.   **127**

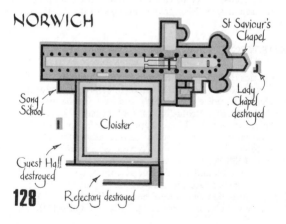

NORWICH

St Saviour's Chapel

Song School

Cloister

Lady Chapel destroyed

Guest Hall destroyed

128   Refectory destroyed

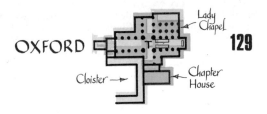

OXFORD **129**

Lady Chapel

Cloister → Chapter House

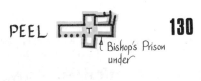

PEEL **130**

✝ Bishop's Prison under

PETERBOROUGH

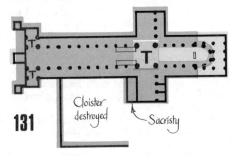

Cloister destroyed

Sacristy

131

OXFORD Christ   Diocese: Berkshire,
                                        Buckinghamshire, Oxfordshire

Augustinian priory originated as nunnery, 735. Church
rebuilt 1158-85; nave curtailed by Wolsey to make space
for quadrangle of Christ Church College (of which it
serves as chapel). Made a cathedral 1542. Unusual Norman arcades having triforium within main arches. Quire
vault with pendants *c.* 1490 (*61*). 14th-c. glass and 15th-c.
stalls in Latin Chapel. Good 17th- and 18th-c. monuments.

PEEL St German
                          Diocese (Sodor & Man): Isle of Man

Ruined cathedral in island castle reputedly founded by
St Patrick, 447. Unroofed in Church-State quarrels of
17th and 18th c. and ineffectually repaired. Bishop's seat
now in chapel of palace at Kirkmichael. Pro-cathedral is
parish church of St George, Douglas.

PETERBOROUGH St Peter, St Paul & St Andrew
                          Diocese: Northamptonshire with the Soke of
                                        Peterborough and Rutland

Benedictine abbey church, created a cathedral 1541.

Rebuilt after disastrous fire 1116-80. Robust Norman
arcades throughout (*4*). 12th-c. wooden ceilings to nave
and transepts, painted with figures in lozenge patterns.
Quire roof 15th c., wood. Grandiose three-arched W
front with small towers, finished by 1238; 15th-c. porch
tucked into its narrow central arch. Fan-vaulted retro-
quire built round Norman apse *c.* 1500. Central tower
rebuilt by Pearson 1882-6.

Monuments of Abbots. Brass lectern late 15th c.
So-called Hedda Stone at E end, a valuable sculpture
of *c.* 800.

Precinct outer gateway medieval. Fragments of abbey
buildings in Bishop's Palace, etc., but cloister walks gone.

PORTSMOUTH   St Thomas of Canterbury
          Diocese: SE Hampshire and the Isle of Wight

Parish church, made a cathedral 1927.

E end pure Early English (*23*). Tower rebuilt after Civil War, also quire with semi-circular arches and a friendly box-pew atmosphere. New nave begun by Nicholson *c.* 1935, to be completed in arena form.

Pulpit 1693. 'Golden Barque' weather-vane 1710.

RIPON   St Peter & St Wilfrid
          Diocese: NW Yorkshire

Monastery founded 660; later collegiate, virtually as pro-cathedral to York. Separate diocese formed 1836.

Complex building history. Tiny 7th-c. crypt beneath central tower. Basically Transitional Norman, with unusual N transept façade, and stately quire arcade combining round and pointed arches. Two partial re-buildings of quire after collapses in 1288 and 1458. Nave and aisles 1502-38, retaining bold 13th-c. W front.

Massive 15th-c. stone pulpitum (inserted to strengthen tower) cuts off quire completely. Good quire stalls *c.* 1490. Rich 14th-c. sedilia.

ROCHESTER   Christ & St. Mary
          Diocese: W Kent

Bishopric founded 604. Monastic (Benedictine) 1082 to 1541.

Nave and aisles mostly of 1178-1240, but E bays began to be rebuilt late in 13th c.; clerestory 15th c. Most of E end (including quire enclosed by solid side walls) mid-13th c., but main S transept and S quire aisle rather later. Early 16th-c. Lady Chapel beyond S aisle. Extensive and unsympathetic 19th-c. restorations, especially of W front. Central tower rebuilt 1905.

13th- and 16th-c. woodwork in quire stalls; 14th-c. wall-painting nearby. Monuments to bishops.

PORTSMOUTH

132

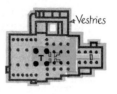

Vestries

RIPON

133

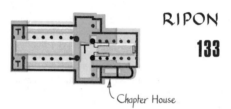

Chapter House

ROCHESTER

134

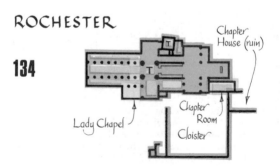

Chapter House (ruin)

Chapter Room

Cloister

Lady Chapel

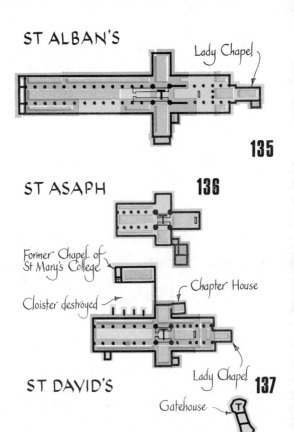

ST ALBAN'S

Lady Chapel

135

ST ASAPH

136

Former Chapel of
St Mary's College

Chapter House

Cloister destroyed

Lady Chapel

ST DAVID'S

137

Gatehouse

ST ALBANS St Alban
Diocese: Bedfordshire and Hertfordshire

Benedictine abbey probably originally founded in 8th c. Parochial since Reformation; a cathedral since 1877.

Basically late 11th c. (*14*), including crossing-tower of Roman brick, and massive nave arcades. Eastward and westward extensions c. 1195-1310. Over-enthusiastic late 19th-c. restoration by Lord Grimthorpe with intractable new W front and transept ends.

Early 13th-c. wall-paintings. Magnificent brass to Abbot Delamere c. 1360. Shrine of St Alban and watching chamber 14th and 15th c. Chantries of Duke Humphrey, 1441, and Abbot Ramryge, 1521.

Great Gateway of abbey 14th c.

ST ASAPH St Asaph
Diocese: Denbighshire, Flintshire, E Merionethshire, and E Montgomeryshire

The smallest cathedral of England and Wales. Monastery founded c. 560 and diocese later. Burnt by English in 13th c. and rebuilt. Quire burnt by Owen Glendower 1402 and rebuilt 1482. Low central tower.

ST DAVIDS St David
Diocese: Cardiganshire, Carmarthenshire and Pembrokeshire

Founded in 6th c. in remote south-west of Wales.

Present building largely of 1180-1200, arches of nave clerestory curiously absorbing the triforium. Quire arches and tower 13th c.; E parts 14th c. Arabic-looking oak nave roof 15th c.

Quire stalls c. 1470, including only Royal stall in a British cathedral. Gower chantry 1347, within earlier pulpitum; Vaughan chantry c. 1520 west of Lady Chapel.

Ruined Bishops' Palace adjoining.

SALISBURY   St Mary
  Diocese: Wiltshire (except extreme N) and Dorset

Rebuilt 1220-60 to supersede cathedral in fortress of Old Sarum.

The most consistent in style of all English cathedrals, almost wholly Early English (*34*), but cloister and chapter house Geometric Decorated (*50*), and graceful 404-foot spire added *c*. 1330. Exterior famous for its perfect massing (*front endpaper*). Interior cool, precise and orderly with lavish use of Purbeck marble (Pl. D).

Fittings and monuments drastically rearranged at Wyatt's 'restoration', 1789. Bishops' monuments include canopied Bridport tomb 1262, fantastic Wyville brass 1375, and Audley chantry 1524. Effigy of William Longespée 1226, the oldest English military figure.

Supremely beautiful close, spaciously green and lined with fascinating houses.

SHEFFIELD   St Peter and St Paul
                                            Diocese: S Yorkshire

Parish church, made a cathedral 1914.

Basically 15th c., with crossing-tower and spire. Nave and transepts rebuilt 1880. Neo-Gothic enlargement begun by Nicholson 1919; intention of turning axis to north-south not realized. Simplified completion by Bailey *c*. 1965, including finishing of N side and addition of W lantern-crossing and angular tower-porch.

16th-c. monuments of Earls of Shrewsbury.

SOUTHWARK   St Saviour
                                    Diocese: S London and E Surrey

Augustinian priory of St Mary Overie founded 1106. Parochial since Reformation and a cathedral since 1905.

Gracious Early English vaulted quire with triforium; four-aisled retro-quire. Nave twice rebuilt in 19th c., latterly by Blomfield 1890-7. Lady Chapel demolished *c*. 1830 for new approach to London Bridge.

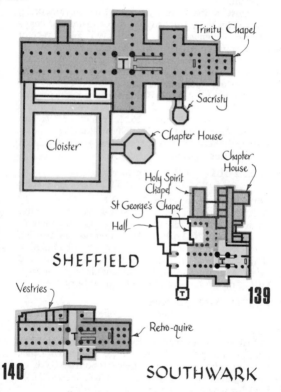

138 SALISBURY

Trinity Chapel

Sacristy

Cloister

Chapter House

Chapter House

Holy Spirit Chapel

St George's Chapel

Hall

SHEFFIELD

139

Vestries

Retro-quire

140 SOUTHWARK

SOUTHWELL **141**

Chapter House

TRURO **142**

Cloister (unfinished)

Chapter Hall

Baptistry

St Mary's Aisle

WAKEFIELD **143**

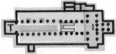

SOUTHWELL St Mary

Diocese: Nottinghamshire

Monastery in existence by 8th c. Church collegiate throughout Middle Ages and until 1840 (like Beverley and Ripon, in effect a pro-cathedral to York). See established 1884.

Basically Norman, begun *c.* 1108. Twin-towered W front, altered in 15th c. (Pl. A). Robust nave arcades; triforium virtually a second storey over aisles. 13th-c. quire resembling Beverley, with triforium and clerestory combined in one unit. Chapter house Geometric Decorated (*90*), with nature carving of the very first quality (*56*).

Rich stone pulpitum completed about 1350, the E and W sides quite different. Early 16th-c. French glass imported after Revolution. Brass eagle lectern from Newstead Abbey, *c.* 1500.

TRURO St Mary

Diocese: Cornwall

Diocese formed 1876.

Elaborate early 16th-c. south aisle of parish church incorporated into new cathedral of 1880-1910; designed by J. L. Pearson in Early English style, but spires, vaults and other detail more French in character. Bare nave, more ornate E end and specially rich baptistry with red porphyry font.

Chapter Hall by John Taylor, 1965 (*86*).

WAKEFIELD All Saints Diocese: SW Yorkshire

Parish church, made a cathedral 1888.

Apparently all 15th c., but nave arcades earlier. N and S fronts rebuilt in 18th and 19th c., and tower with 247-foot spire 1858. New transept and vaulted chancel by F. L. Pearson, 1904.

15th-c. stalls. Screen 1635. Organ case 1743.

WELLS   St Andrew
                              Diocese (Bath & Wells): Somerset

Diocese founded 909.

Present cathedral commenced about 1186 and consecrated 1239; E end remodelled in 14th c. (*49*). Exceptional W front with 400 statues in niches; W towers 15th c.   Noble 14th-c. central tower with buttressing 'scissor' arches. Interior rich with clustered columns and foliage capitals (*22*).

Much 14th-c. glass at E end, including Jesse window. Very early Renaissance pulpit *c*. 1530. Fine desk lectern, 1660. Astronomical clock with performing figures, *c*. 1390. Unusual 15th-c. stone screen to N transept. Two splendid 15th-c. chantries in nave.

Lierne-vaulted cloister mostly 15th c.   Moated Bishop's Palace begun in 13th c. Graceful octagonal chapter house with famous branching stair. Link over medieval bridge (Chain Gate) with 14th-c. Vicars' Close.

WINCHESTER   Holy Trinity
    Diocese: Hampshire (except SE) and Channel Islands

Founded before 650. The longest of all medieval cathedrals.

Powerful transepts of *c*. 1080, the most complete English building of the period remaining (*5*). Contemporary nave arcades and aisles altered and encased late in 14th c.; intricate vaults (*59*), but timid W front. Retro-quire and Lady Chapel *c*. 1200; 15th-c. vaults at E end. Quire early 16th c., retaining 14th-c. arches.

Rich furnishings. Six magnificent chantry chapels: Edington and Wykeham in nave, 1366 and 1404, Beaufort and Waynflete (*92*) in retro-quire, 1447 and 1486, Fox and Gardiner in quire, 1528 and 1525. Splendid square Norman black marble font. 14th-c. stalls.

Ruined Norman chapter house. Wolvesey Palace nearby, for centuries the home of bishops.

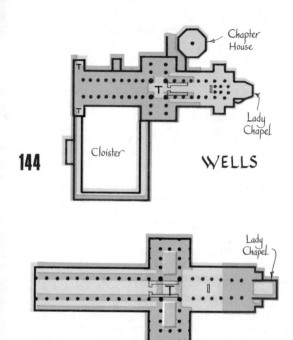

144

Chapter House

T

T

T

Cloister

T

Lady Chapel

WELLS

145

Lady Chapel

T

Library over

Chapter House destroyed

WINCHESTER

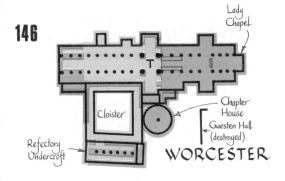

146

Lady Chapel

T

Cloister

Chapter House

Guesten Hall (destroyed)

Refectory Undercroft

WORCESTER

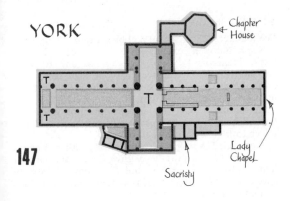

YORK

Chapter House

T

T

T

Lady Chapel

Sacristy

147

I

WORCESTER Christ and St Mary

Diocese: Worcestershire

Bishopric founded late in 7th c. Monastic (Benedictine) from 10th c. till 16th c.

Eastern parts (*37*) beautifully rebuilt from 1224 onwards, rich with Purbeck marble and stiff-leaf carving and retaining impressive 11th-c. crypt. Western half with transepts still Norman in outline but rebuilt piecemeal: strange Transitional western bays (*19*), but remainder mostly 14th c., and astonishingly uniform with quire. Central tower fell 1175; not rebuilt till 1374. Exterior soullessly refaced by Perkins and Scott, 1857-74.

· Richly pinnacled Prince Arthur's Chantry 1504. Tomb of King John *c.* 1530, with superb effigy of *c.* 1230. 14th-c. misericords built into 19th-c. stalls.

Circular Norman chapter house. Cloister mostly 14th c.; refectory with Norman undercroft. Other monastic remains. Bishop's Palace substantially 13th c.

YORK St Peter

Diocese: E Yorkshire

See founded 627; made an archbishopric not long after.

Slight Norman remains in crypt and central tower piers. Transepts 1227-60, with rose window to south (*30*) and noble Five Sisters, 53-foot high lancets, to north. Nave, the widest in England, rebuilt 1291-*c.* 1350; unusually elaborate W front. Retro-quire 1361-70 and quire proper 1380-1400; E transepts not projecting beyond quire aisles; W towers and very grand central tower 15th c. Main vaults all of wood.

More medieval glass than in any other English cathedral: 13th-c. grisaille in Five Sisters and chapter house, 14th-c. W window, and E window of 1408 all specially notable. Late 15th-c. pulpitum. Many fine monuments in eastern parts.

Chapter house Geometric, unique for gallery below windows.

FORMER CATHEDRALS OF ENGLAND AND WALES

Dioceses have been continually reorganized through the centuries, and thus many towns and villages have some traces or tradition of cathedrals which no longer exist.

A. Abbeys, priories and collegiate churches:

Chester (St John). A collegiate church of cathedral status from 1075-95; massive nave of that date still used by parish, but quire and tower ruined.

Osney Oxfordshire. Priory church used as a cathedral from 1542-6; hardly a vestige remains.

In addition the following are described in Chapter 5:

Bath, Somerset	Hexham, Northumberland
Crediton, Devon	St German's, Cornwall
Dorchester, Oxfordshire	Sherborne, Dorset
Glastonbury, Somerset	Westminster

B. The following all have fragmentary remains of former cathedrals:

Coventry Warwickshire. As well as the ruin of the 15th-c. parish-church cathedral, some slight remains not far away of the earlier cathedral. See p. 90.

Denbigh. Leicester's church is an unfinished shell of 1579, originally intended to become a cathedral.

North Elmham Norfolk (2). Remains of a Saxon cathedral within a castle, somewhat confused by its conversion into a house in the Middle Ages. The seat of East Anglian bishops from *c.* 670 till 1070.

Old Sarum Wiltshire. Complete foundations of Norman cathedral of St Osmund within a hill-fort. Consecrated 1092; see transferred to Salisbury (New Sarum) about 1225.

C. The exact sites of the following are unknown (the dates are those when the dioceses existed):

Chester-le-Street Durham 875-995.

Dunwich Suffolk 630-955. Swallowed up by the sea.

Leicester 679-874. Possibly where one of the present parish churches now stands.

Lindisfarne Northumberland (Holy Island) 635-875, i.e. much older than the present priory ruin.

Lindsey Lincolnshire *c.* 680-*c.* 875.

Selsey Sussex 680-1080. Probably now under the sea.

Thetford Norfolk 1075-1091. Not on the site of the priory ruin.

D. **Ramsbury** Wiltshire. The church of the Holy Cross was a cathedral from 909 till 1058, but nothing of the present building is recognizably so old.

5 ABBEYS AND PRIORIES OF ENGLAND AND WALES

BATH ABBEY   Somerset   St Peter & St Paul

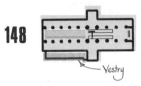

148

Not really an abbey, but a priory; once co-cathedral with Wells and still linked with it in Bishop's title.

Rebuilding began 1499; much smaller than before but grand and uniform in style (65). Tall clerestory and no triforium. Fan vaults not finally completed till 19th c. Carved ladders with angels on W front buttresses.

Wall-tablets and other memorials in vast profusion.

BEVERLEY MINSTER   Yorkshire
St John of Beverley

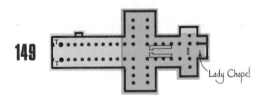

149

Traditionally founded in 8th c. and made collegiate by King Athelstan in 10th c. In the Middle Ages virtually a pro-cathedral to York, like Ripon and Southwell.

Quire, aisles and transepts *c.* 1225-45. Nave and aisles *c.* 1340, matching E end in general design but not in detail. Twin-towered W front 15th c., the finest of its period in England.

Sixty-eight quire stalls of *c.* 1525. Exuberant 14th-c. monument to Lady Idoine Percy.

BINHAM PRIORY Norfolk   St Mary

Benedictine. Norman nave. Sadly mutilated Geometric Decorated W front, even earlier than Westminster. Quire destroyed.

BOLTON PRIORY Yorkshire
St Cuthbert & St Mary

Augustinian. Nave and N aisle mostly 13th c. and ruined quire 14th c. Tower 1520. Specially picturesque situation by River Wharfe.

BOXGROVE PRIORY Sussex
St Mary & St Blaise

Benedictine. Quire *c.* 1220, very like Chichester. Nave *c.* 1170, destroyed except two bays. Low central tower. Rich de la Warr chantry 1526.

BRIDLINGTON PRIORY Yorkshire St Mary

Augustinian, founded 1113. Stately twin-towered nave now parochial, 13th c., but with beginnings of Perpendicular conversion (*68*). Gatehouse, called the Bayle.

BUILDWAS ABBEY Shropshire

Cistercian. 12th-c. church and monastic buildings, simple and noble but entirely ruined.

BYLAND ABBEY Yorkshire

Cistercian, all ruined. Large church late 12th c., and extensive monastic buildings. Noted water-leaf capitals. Original floor tiling.

CARTMEL PRIORY Lancashire   St Mary

Augustinian. Quire and nave largely *c.* 1200 but with
later windows, etc. Odd central tower with top stage
set diagonally. 17th-c. stalls and screen. 14th-c. Har-
rington tomb.

CASTLE ACRE PRIORY Norfolk

Cluniac, entirely ruined. Begun *c.* 1100; rich Norman
W front. Early 16th-c. prior's house, roofed.

ST BOTOLPH'S PRIORY COLCHESTER
Essex

Augustinian. Impressive ruin of church nave and W
front, *c.* 1100. Fine doorways.

CREDITON CHURCH Devon   Holy Cross

Collegiate till Reformation but from 909 to 1050 the
seat of a bishop. Transepts and crossing 12th c.; Lady
Chapel *c.* 1300; remainder mostly 15th c.

CROWLAND ABBEY Lincolnshire

Benedictine. Vaulted 15th-c. N aisle preserved as parish
church; remainder ruined, partly Norman.

DOWNSIDE ABBEY Somerset

Benedictine, established 1814. Cathedral-like church
begun 1872, still incomplete: transepts by Hansom and
nave by Sir Giles Gilbert Scott.

CHRISTCHURCH PRIORY Hampshire

Holy Trinity

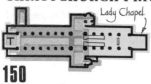

Lady Chapel

150

Priory refounded by Augustinians 1150. Norman nave and transepts with richly ornamented stair on north. Quire with aisles early 16th c. W tower early 15th c. Lady Chapel, with upper floor of unknown purpose.

Main reredos 14th c. Stalls with misericords c. 1525, with some Renaissance detail. Several chantries, especially Countess of Salisbury's, 1541.

DORCHESTER ABBEY Oxfordshire

St Peter & St Paul

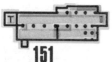

151

Augustinian. Cathedral from 7th c. till 1092 when bishop moved to Lincoln; now parish church. Nave 11th or 12th c., probably on earlier foundation. Remainder mostly Decorated. E window in form of Jesse tree of stone and glass. W tower 1602.

DORE ABBEY Herefordshire

Holy Trinity & St Mary

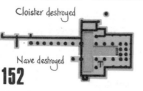

Cloister destroyed

Nave destroyed

152

Cistercian. Eastern parts restored in 17th c. as parish church; nave and monastic buildings mostly gone. Crossing and transepts Transitional Norman, c. 1180. Rich quire and retroquire Early English, c. 1210. Tower and much woodwork of 1633.

DUNSTABLE PRIORY   Bedfordshire   St Peter

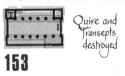

Quire and Transepts destroyed

153

Augustinian, founded 1131. Wide Norman nave now parish church. Present clerestory formed by great arches of former gallery. Rich 13th-c. NW doorway.

FOUNTAINS ABBEY   Yorkshire

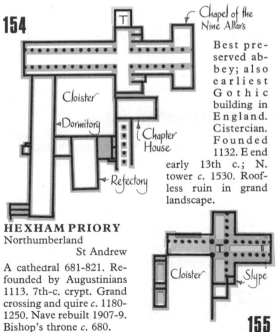

154

Chapel of the Nine Altars

Cloister

Dormitory

Chapter House

Refectory

Best preserved abbey; also earliest Gothic building in England. Cistercian. Founded 1132. E end early 13th c.; N. tower *c.* 1530. Roofless ruin in grand landscape.

HEXHAM PRIORY
Northumberland
                St Andrew

A cathedral 681-821. Refounded by Augustinians 1113. 7th-c. crypt. Grand crossing and quire *c.* 1180-1250. Nave rebuilt 1907-9. Bishop's throne *c.* 680.

Cloister

Slype

155

FURNESS ABBEY   Lancashire

Cistercian, a red sandstone ruin of late 12th c. and later dates. Extensive domestic buildings.

GLASTONBURY ABBEY   Somerset

Benedictine, the facts and legends of its origins inextricably lost. Church, 590 feet long, almost disappeared. Western Lady Chapel rich late Norman, *c.* 1185. Octagonal-roofed Abbot's Kitchen *c.* 1440.

HOWDEN MINSTER   Yorkshire

Made collegiate 1265. Nave and aisles approaching Decorated style like York. Quire and aisles fully developed Decorated. Central tower and chapter house Prependicular. Now parochial; E end ruined since 1696.

KIRKSTALL ABBEY   Yorkshire

Cistercian. Transitional Norman of *c.* 1150-75, little altered. Roofless, but remarkably complete including domestic buildings. Good W portal.

LANERCOST PRIORY   Cumberland
St Mary Magdalen

Augustinian, founded *c.* 1166. Nave and N aisle parochial; E end roofless. Mostly early 13th c. W range of domestic buildings well preserved.

LEOMINSTER PRIORY   Herefordshire
St Peter & St Paul

Benedictine. 12th-c. red sandstone nave now parish church. S aisle largely 14th c. with lavish ballflower-ornamented windows. Quire and monastic buildings destroyed.

LLANTHONY PRIORY Monmouthshire

Augustinian. Extensive church ruins *c.* 1200. Remains of gatehouse and other monastic buildings, some incorporated into hotel.

LONDON: PRIORY of St Bartholomew the Great

Augustinian, founded 1123. Nave destroyed. Norman quire forms parish church. 14th-c. Lady Chapel.

MILTON ABBEY Dorset

Benedictine, founded 938. Church exquisitely set in park and woods, now used as School chapel. Quire and aisles and S transept 14th c.; N transept and tower 15th c.; nave destroyed.

MOUNT GRACE PRIORY Yorkshire

Carthusian, better-preserved than other English Charterhouses. Ruined small church and great cloister with individual monks' dwellings.

OTTERY ST MARY CHURCH Devon
St Mary

Made collegiate 1337 and then virtually rebuilt as small-scale version of Exeter Cathedral, with transeptal towers and eastern Lady Chapel. Outer N. aisle *c.* 1520, fan-vaulted.

PERSHORE ABBEY Worcestershire Holy Cross

Benedictine. Early 13th-c. quire and transepts. Nave and Lady Chapel destroyed; E apse of 1847. 14th-c. central tower. Rich arcades with combined triforium and clerestory (*43*).

MALMESBURY ABBEY Wiltshire

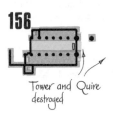

156

Tower and Quire destroyed

Benedictine, founded in 7th c. Church rebuilt *c.* 1160-70; nave became parochial at Dissolution; remainder, once boasting a steeple higher than Salisbury's, left to ruin. Norman (*8*) but with pointed arches (*18*). Clerestory and nave vault 14th c. Excellent 12th-c. ornament and figure sculpture in S porch.

MALVERN PRIORY Worcestershire

St Mary & St Michael

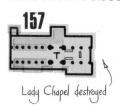

157

Lady Chapel destroyed

Benedictine, probably founded 1085. Norman nave arcades, but remainder mostly *c.* 1420-60. Bought by town at Dissolution, becoming parochial. 15th-c. glass the finest in England, rich in browns, blues and yellows. Also the only medieval wall-tiling in England.

ROMSEY ABBEY Hampshire

St Mary & St Ethelfleda

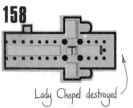

158

Lady Chapel destroyed

Benedictine nunnery founded 907. Church bought by town at Dissolution, for parochial use. Built *c.* 1120-1230, but W end 13th c. Norman arcades and triforium, hesitant and inconsistent in detail; clerestory largely 13th c. Very plain tower. 11th-c. Romsey Rood by S transept.

SELBY ABBEY Yorkshire
Christ, St Mary & St German

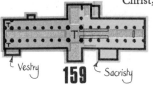

Benedictine, founded 1069. Church still complete and used by parish. Nave Norman and Early English, well contrasted. Transepts Norman;

E end Decorated (*41*).

SHERBORNE ABBEY Dorset   St Mary

Benedictine, founded as cathedral 705; bishop moved to Old Sarum 1075. Church taken over by parish at Reformation. Norman, converted to Perpendicular (*64*). Superb fan-vaulting in nave and quire. Monastic buildings absorbed into School.

TEWKESBURY ABBEY Gloucestershire
St Mary

Benedictine. Great church, now parochial, complete except Lady Chapel. Norman nave: giant western arch and 14th-c. vault. Quire similar. 14th-c. chevet. Tran-

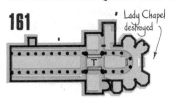

septs and tower Norman. Warwick, Despencer and other chantries. Organ in part *c.* 1600. Abbey gatehouse.

QUARR ABBEY Hampshire (Isle of Wight)

Benedictine, refounded 1907. Church 1911-12 by Bellot, all brick with impressive and original arch construction. Medieval Cistercian ruins.

RIEVAULX ABBEY Yorkshire

Cistercian. An unspoilt ruin, wonderfully complete. Church finished *c.* 1150 (*25*) but E end rebuilt *c.* 1225-40. Splendid quire. Monastic buildings well preserved and easily understandable.

ST GERMAN'S PRIORY Cornwall

Augustinian. Bishop's seat until 1050. Twin-towered nave and aisles rebuilt subsequently, mostly Norman and now parochial. Quire destroyed.

STRATA FLORIDA ABBEY Cardiganshire

Cistercian, founded 1164. Church finished early in 13th c., now completely ruined. Fine W doorway.

THORNEY ABBEY County of Huntingdon & Peterborough St Mary & St Botolph

Benedictine. Nave only of late 11th-c. church, restored for parish use 1638. Aisles gone; arcades like Ely.

TINTERN ABBEY Monmouthshire

Cistercian, founded 1131. Remarkably well preserved ruin of Decorated church and earlier monastic buildings.

VALLE CRUCIS ABBEY Denbighshire

Cistercian, founded *c.* 1200. Beautifully situated ruin, 13th c. Square 14th-c. chapter house, complete.

WALTHAM ABBEY Essex
Holy Cross & St Lawrence

Augustinian. Norman nave now parish church, with massive grooved piers like Durham (7). W tower 1556-8. Eastern and monastic parts not preserved.

WENLOCK ABBEY Shropshire

Cluniac, mostly Early English and entirely ruined. Rich Norman chapter house.

WHITBY ABBEY Yorkshire

Benedictine, founded 657. Cliff-top church ruin almost all 13th c.; impressive E front with lancets.

WORKSOP PRIORY Nottinghamshire
St Cuthbert & St Mary

Augustinian, founded 1103. Norman nave now parochial; transepts reconstructed: elegant 13th-c. Lady Chapel next to S transept; remainder gone except 14th-c. gatehouse.

WYMONDHAM ABBEY Norfolk
St Mary & St Thomas à Becket

Benedictine, founded 1107. Grand Norman nave now parish church. Two 15th-c. towers, at W end and at crossing. Quire ruined.

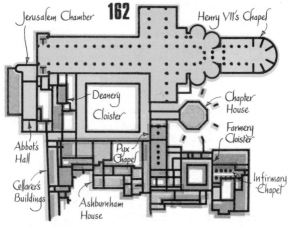

162

Jerusalem Chamber — Henry VII's Chapel — Deanery Cloister — Chapter House — Farmery Cloister — Abbot's Hall — Pyx Chapel — Infirmary Chapel — Cellarer's Buildings — Ashburnham House

WIMBORNE MINSTER Dorset   St Cuthburga

163

Royal chapel and college founded 1043. Parochial. Mostly late Norman, 13th-c. E end with crypt under. 14th-c. astronomical clock. Chained library founded 1686.

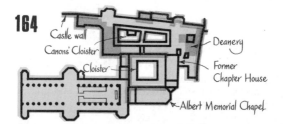

164

Castle wall — Canons' Cloister — Cloister — Deanery — Former Chapter House — Albert Memorial Chapel

WESTMINSTER ABBEY London   St Peter

(*162*) Benedictine; early history obscure. A cathedral from 1540-50 only. Survival due to unique status as royal coronation and burial church.

Some 12th-c. monastic buildings remaining. Church reconstruction begun 1245, French Geometric in character (extensively based on Reims) (*52*): hence unusual internal height and profusion of flying buttresses. Building work interrupted on completion of quire and five bays of nave, 1269; resumed 1375, still, astonishingly, in same style. Eastern (Henry VII's) Chapel 1503-12, unparalleled for wealth of sculpture and intricacy of vaults. W towers by Hawksmoor 1734, Gothic.

Monuments without number, typifying every period and taste, often wantonly discordant with the building. 13th-c. Italian marble floors. Coronation chair.

Splendid chapter house 1245-50. Cloisters mostly late 14th c. Ancillary buildings, now largely domestic.

ST GEORGE'S CHAPEL, WINDSOR
  Berkshire

(*164*) The Chapel of the Order of the Garter, with a college of Dean and Canons. Within the castle walls.

1475-1511, rich late Gothic (*63, 67*). Complex broad main vault merging with clerestory. Aisles fan-vaulted. Central tower never built.

Royal pew originated as watching chamber of Edward IV's Chantry. Canopied stalls in three tiers, for Knights of the Garter, canons and choir, c. 1480; unique display of heraldic plates and banners above. W window with mostly original glass.

Horseshoe Cloister of 21 houses for former priest-vicars c. 1480, on W side. Canons' houses and cloister to north. Garter Chapter House now part of Deanery.

Albert Memorial Chapel to east, c. 1350, now virtually a Victorian shrine.

K

6 ROMAN CATHOLIC CATHEDRALS OF ENGLAND AND WALES

Arundel Sussex, Diocese of Arundel & Brighton, St Philip Neri. 1870-73 by J. A. Hansom & Son, in French Gothic like Beauvais in miniature. Became a cathedral 1965.

Birmingham Warwickshire St Chad. 1839-41 by A. Pugin, red brick in 14th-c. Baltic German Gothic style. NW chapel 1933; other additions 1964. 16th-c. Flemish pulpit. German carvings in screen, throne and stalls. Good 19th-c. glass.

Brentwood Essex Sacred Heart & St Helen. 1861 by Blount, with polygonal steeple, unprepossessing. Became a cathedral 1917.

Cardiff Glamorgan St David. 1884-7 by Peter Paul Pugin, with unusually wide nave. Became a cathedral 1916. Badly bombed 1941, and restored.

Clifton Gloucestershire Holy Apostles. 1839 by Goodridge in Greek style with unfinished giant columns all round. Redesigned 1847-8 by Hansom with Lombardic Gothic details (*81*). New cathedral by Sir Percy Thomas & Son planned on nearby site.

Lancaster Lancashire St Peter. 1859 by Paley, in Geometric style on large scale. Became a cathedral 1924.

Leeds Yorkshire St Anne. Diocese 1878. Rebuilt 1902-4 by Eastwood (*82*). S Chapel reredos by Pugin.

Liverpool Lancashire Christ the King. Splendid brick crypt of Lutyens' unfinished cathedral, *c.* 1930. Completed 1962-7 by Gibberd in form of gigantic concrete-framed wigwam, capped with blue-glazed lantern and fibreglass-pinnacled crown. Central altar and peripheral chapels (*85, 165*).

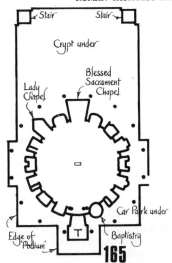

Middlesbrough Yorkshire St Mary. 1872 by Goldie & Child, red brick. Became a cathedral 1878.

Newcastle Northumberland, Diocese of Hexham & Newcastle, St Mary. 1844 by Pugin in Decorated style. Exterior enhanced by 222-foot spire by Hansom, 1860-73.

Northampton Northamptonshire   St Mary & St Thomas. Begun by Pugin 1844. Nave and aisles added by E. W. Pugin 1863. Brick crossing-tower, transepts and E end by Herbert 1948-55.

Nottingham Nottinghamshire St Barnabas. 1842-44 by Pugin with good 150-foot steeple and 76 windows of his design.

Plymouth Devon, St Mary & St Boniface. 1858, by Hansom in Early English style.

Portsmouth Hampshire St John the Evangelist. 1877-82 by Crawley. Dark red brick in Decorated style, well proportioned and delicate. Later additions by Hansom 1886-92 and Scoles. Became a cathedral 1882.

Salford Lancashire St John. 1855, by Weightman & Hadfield in Decorated style with tall crossing-steeple.

Shrewsbury Shropshire Our Lady Help of Christians & St Peter of Alcantara. 1856 by E. W. Pugin; impressively tall Decorated.

Southwark London St George. 1840-8 by Pugin; altered after 1941 bombing, by Romilly Craze.

Westminster London The Most Precious Holy Blood, St Mary, St Joseph and St Peter. 1895-1903 by Bentley in Byzantine style with domed crossing and nave (*166*). Italianate campanile 284 feet high. Stations of the Cross by Eric Gill *c.* 1914.

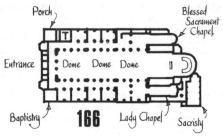

166

Wrexham Denbighshire, Diocese of Menevia, Our Lady of Sorrows. 1857, by E. W. Pugin in Decorated style; parish-church size with stone spire.

Scottish cathedrals fall into three groups: first, medieval buildings which, as in England, were the seats of Roman Catholic bishops but which either fell to ruin at the Reformation (like Elgin) or have been maintained as places of worship (like Glasgow) by the Presbyterian Church; secondly, the comparatively modern Roman Catholic cathedrals of the new hierarchy established in 1878 (the Reformation never quite eliminated Catholicism in the remoter parts); and, thirdly, the bishops' seats of the Episcopal Church of Scotland (in conflict with the Presbyterians for three centuries until 1864) which is organized like the Church of England.

The earliest sculptured remains show Celtic influence (knobby and interlaced patterns, dragons, etc.), (*168*); the round tower of Brechin (its exact purpose is unknown) is like many to be found in Ireland (*167*). The Romanesque and thirteenth century work are very similar to the English, good examples being the abbeys of Dunfermline and Jedburgh. A distinct time-lag is, however, noticeable: Glasgow's quire, for example, whose lancet style is based on Salisbury, is a decade or two later. Foliage ornament is much more rigid in style than English. Windows in the fifteenth century increased in size to a less extent than in England and the Decorated style led into one that was more akin to continental Flamboyant than to English Perpendicular. This was largely because of the political ties with France at that period. Polygonal east ends were reintroduced. Even Portuguese influence is traceable in the fantastic sculptures of the collegiate church of Rosslyn.

Religious quarrels forbade the possibility of further cathedral-building until the nineteenth century. Many churches for both the Episcopalians and the Roman Catholics were designed by local architects of the Gothic Revival, but there are instances of the work of Butterfield, Gilbert Scott, Street and Comper.

167 ROUND TOWER
BRECHIN
c. 1000

ST JOHN'S CROSS
IONA c. 950

168

DRAGON CAPITAL,
S · ARCADE IONA
c. 1150

169

KIRKWALL
c. 1180

170

TOP OF TOWER
LATER, c. 1250

W · END OF
QUIRE

E · END OF
NAVE

N · TRANSEPT

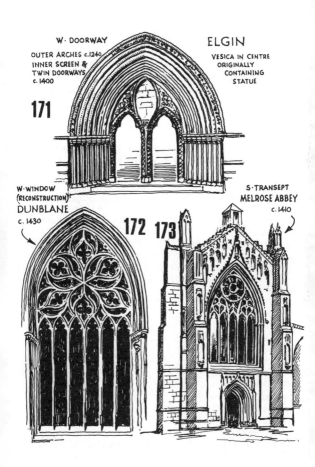

W· DOORWAY

OUTER ARCHES c.1240
INNER SCREEN &
TWIN DOORWAYS
c.1400

171

ELGIN

VESICA IN CENTRE
ORIGINALLY
CONTAINING
STATUE

W· WINDOW
(RECONSTRUCTION)
DUNBLANE
c.1430

172

173

S· TRANSEPT
MELROSE ABBEY
c.1410

ANCIENT CATHEDRALS OF SCOTLAND

(Unless completely ruined, they are used for worship by the United Established Church of Scotland (Presbyterian); all are thus no longer cathedrals.)

Aberdeen Aberdeenshire St Machar. Founded *c.* 1150. Transepts ruined and quire never completed; crossing *c.* 1360; 7-bay nave *c.* 1430; roof and W steeples *c.* 1530.

Birnie Moray. Cathedral of diocese of Moray *c.* 1180-1203. 12th-c. nave and chancel.

Brechin Angus. Founded *c.* 1150 on site of earlier abbey. 87-foot round tower (*167*); nave 13th c.; W tower 14th c.; quire and transepts mostly 1900-2.

Dunblane Perthshire St Blane & St Laurence (*174*). Founded *c.* 1150. Mostly *c.* 1240 but base of tower earlier; nave long in ruins, re-roofed 1893 (*172*).

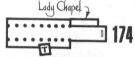

Dunkeld Perthshire. Abbey founded 815 and cathedral *c.* 1120. Roofless nave and aisles 1406-64, with Flamboyant tracery; tower *c.* 1490; 14th-c. quire used as church; chapter house *c.* 1460 now mausoleum of Dukes of Atholl.

Edinburgh Midlothian St Giles (*175*). Made collegiate 1466; a cathedral only for short periods in 17th c. From Reformation till 1872 divided into several separate churches. Mostly *c.* 1390-1450; vaulted quire; tower with open crown *c.* 1495; Chapel of the Thistle 1911 (Lorimer).

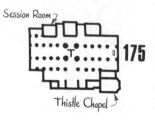

Elgin Moray (*176*). The 'Lanthorn of the North', founded 1224 (Pl. H). Wantonly destroyed after

Reformation. Handsome W front (*171*) with late 14th-c. towers.

Glasgow Lanarkshire St Mungo (*177*). Founded 1123. The most complete great medieval church in Scotland. Extensive crypt or 'Laigh Kirk'; 225-foot spire c. 1420.

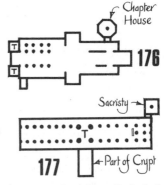

Iona Argyll St Mary. Monastery founded by St Columba 563.

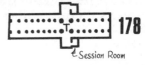

Burial place of Scottish kings till 11th c. Cathedral (diocese of Sodor) 1499-1578. Mostly early 16th c., restored from ruin in 20th c. (*168*, *169*).

Kirkwall Orkney St Magnus (*178*). Founded 1137. Till 1472 under archbishopric of Trondhjem (Norway).

Mainly severe Romanesque (*170*), later extended east and west. Nave restored from semi-ruin 1912-20.

St Andrew's Fife. Founded 1160, consecrated 1318; the largest cathedral in Scotland. Utterly ruined except parts of W and E ends and of S wall of nave.

Spynie Moray. Cathedral of diocese of Moray 1203-24. Destroyed 1736; but churchyard remains.

Major Scottish abbeys, with churches as large as the cathedrals, are Arbroath (Angus), Dryburgh (Berwickshire), Dunfermline (Fife), Holyrood (Midlothian), Jedburgh, Kelso and Melrose (*173*) (all Roxburghshire), Paisley (Renfrewshire) and Sweetheart (Dumfriesshire).

CATHEDRALS OF THE SCOTTISH EPISCOPAL CHURCH

(names of architects in brackets)

Aberdeen, Diocese of Aberdeen & Orkneys, St Andrew. Early Gothic Revival—imitation Perpendicular—1817; chancel 1880 (Street).

Dundee, Diocese of Brechin, St Paul 1852-5, with 220-foot spire (Gilbert Scott).

Edinburgh St Mary 1874-9, with central 276-foot spire (Gilbert Scott).

Glasgow, Diocese of Glasgow & Galloway, St Mary 1870-1; 205-foot spire of 1892-3 (Gilbert Scott).

Inverness, Diocese of Moray, Ross & Caithness, St Andrew 1866-9 (Alexander Ross); angel font copied from Thorvaldsen's at Copenhagen cathedral.

Millport, Diocese of Argyll & the Isles, Holy Spirit. On Great Cumbrae island; begun 1849 (Butterfield) and still incomplete. Oban, St John the Divine, is co-cathedral, 1863-82.

Perth, Diocese of St Andrew's, Dunkeld & Dunblane, St Ninian 1850-90 (Butterfield).

ROMAN CATHOLIC CATHEDRALS IN SCOTLAND

Aberdeen St Mary of the Assumption 1860-80; 200-foot spire.

Ayr, Diocese of Galloway, The Good Shepherd.

Dundee, Diocese of Dunkeld, St Andrew. Begun 1836.

Edinburgh, Archbishopric of St Andrew's & Edinburgh, St Mary 1813-14 (Gillespie Graham).

Glasgow, Archbishopric, St Andrew. Originally of 1797, but present building begun 1866.

Motherwell Our Lady of Good Aid. Begun 1873; seat of bishop since 1947.

Oban, Diocese of Argyll & the Isles, St Columba 1932 (Giles Gilbert Scott).

Paisley St Mirin 1808.

In Ireland Roman Catholicism has always survived strongly, Henry VIII's supremacy over the Church only being conceded by a minority. The ancient cathedrals, many of them now in ruins, belong to the Protestant Church of Ireland, disestablished in 1869. The oldest Catholic ones are of the period just before 1829, the year of 'emancipation'; Waterford, for example, dates from 1793-6 and is by the same architect as the Protestant cathedral in the same city. The newest, that of Galway, was only consecrated in 1965.

As in England and Wales, little pre-Romanesque building is left standing, and the dating of what there is is extremely difficult; an instance is the nave of Glendalough, which may be early ninth century. Romanesque work takes on similar characteristics to that of other countries but the influence of Celtic ornament is never far below the surface (*181*). Round towers were built in the tenth to twelfth centuries for defence and look-outs, hanging bells, and as guides to indicate a church. Though small, Cashel cathedral (*179*) is one of the most moving, on a fortified rock in the midst of a plain.

Even the greater medieval cathedrals, such as Christ Church (*180*) and St Patrick's (both in Dublin), Kilkenny and Limerick, are modest in scale, while the smaller ones are simple cross-shaped buildings. Clerestories are rare; so are crypts. A kind of flowing tracery (as in Scotland) was used instead of Perpendicular patterns; otherwise little is distinctively Irish.

Several Protestant cathedrals have seventeenth- and eighteenth-century work; notable are Lismore (1633), the nave of Derry, built by the Corporation of London in 1628-33, Waterford (1773) and Downpatrick (1790-1827). In the nineteenth century the English architect Street practically rebuilt Kildare, as well as St Patrick's Cathedral, Dublin; Cork (1864-79) is the masterpiece of his contemporary, William Burges.

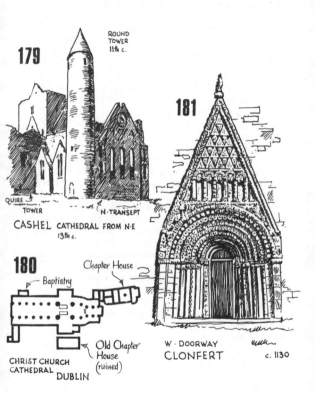

179

ROUND
TOWER
11th c.

QUIRE
TOWER

N·TRANSEPT

CASHEL CATHEDRAL FROM N·E
13th c.

180

Baptistry

Chapter House

Old Chapter
House
(ruined)

CHRIST CHURCH
CATHEDRAL
DUBLIN

181

W·DOORWAY
CLONFERT

c. 1130

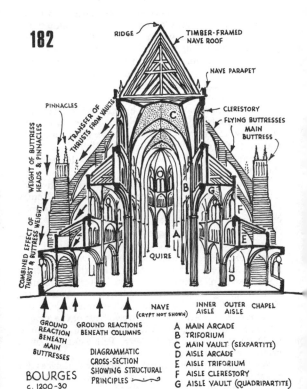

182

RIDGE

TIMBER-FRAMED NAVE ROOF

NAVE PARAPET

PINNACLES

TRANSFER OF THRUSTS FROM VAULTS

WEIGHT OF BUTTRESS HEADS & PINNACLES

COMBINED EFFECT OF THRUST & BUTTRESS WEIGHT

CLERESTORY

FLYING BUTTRESSES

MAIN BUTTRESS

C

B

G

A

F

E

D

QUIRE

GROUND REACTION BENEATH MAIN BUTTRESSES

GROUND REACTIONS BENEATH COLUMNS

NAVE (CRYPT NOT SHOWN)

INNER AISLE

OUTER AISLE

CHAPEL

A MAIN ARCADE
B TRIFORIUM
C MAIN VAULT (SEXPARTITE)
D AISLE ARCADE
E AISLE TRIFORIUM
F AISLE CLERESTORY
G AISLE VAULT (QUADRIPARTITE)

DIAGRAMMATIC CROSS-SECTION SHOWING STRUCTURAL PRINCIPLES

BOURGES
c. 1200-30

FRENCH ROMANESQUE, up to 1140

In France the round-arched style was more consciously a survival than a revival of Roman ways of building, but many more regional variations exist than in Britain, partly because of the split into warring provinces.

In Burgundy, for example, Roman motifs were perpetuated with fluted arches and tunnel-vaults. Apart from its pointed arcades, the interior of Autun (183) is virtually classical in conception.

Provence had tall narrow churches with even more classical detail (Pl. M) with pointed tunnel-vaults and with very narrow aisles if any. Cloisters were a special feature of the churches of the south (184).

Poitou had hall-churches, that is with aisles as tall as the naves.

The province of Aquitaine was distinguished by majestic domed churches recalling the halls of Roman *thermae*. Angoulême (195, Pl. N) is a splendid example; originally it had towers on both transepts.

The vaults and walling of the Auvergne are notable for the use of variously coloured volcanic stones.

In Normandy the Romanesque style was developed towards the form we know in England, with the basilican (long, aisled) plan terminating in an eastern ambulatory with radiating chapels. The Abbaye-aux-Hommes (St Etienne) at Caen has sexpartite vaults over huge square nave bays each corresponding to two bays of the arcades and aisles, producing the same slow solemn rhythm as at Durham a few decades later. Rib vaults followed groin vaults as in England.

Western towers originated as structural devices for resisting the thrust of the nave arcades; Strasbourg, *c*. 1015, may be the earliest instance.

Portals had highly developed carving and were often divided into two openings by a *trumeau*; the carved saints became long and stylized with small heads (186).

POINTED ARCHES & QUADRI-PARTITE VAULTS **183**

NAVE ARCADE AUTUN c. 1120

PILASTERS OF CLASSICAL TYPE WITH FIGURE-CARVING ON CAPITALS

CLOISTER ARCADE AIX-EN-PROVENCE c. 1080 **184**

ROUND ARCHES AND DOUBLE COLUMNS

DOME

PENDENTIVE

185

SQUARE NAVE BAYS VAULTED WITH A SERIES OF DOMES

NAVE PERIGUEUX c. 1140

TYMPANUM

186 W. PORTAL ARLES c. 1150

FRENCH EARLY GOTHIC, *circa* 1140 to 1180

The royal counsellor Abbot Suger of Saint Denis is credited with the invention of the Gothic style, but only a few years before it first appeared in England at the abbeys of Roche and Fountains; of his work at Saint Denis only the quire (*188*) and the west front survive.

Under Louis VII (1137-80) the Île-de-France, centred on Paris, became a gradually more powerful nucleus of a united French kingdom; for a century and a half it was to remain the centre of the most inspired structural creativity the world has ever known. Masons and sculptors, artists in glass, paint and tapestry, workers in wood and metals, looked to the Île-de-France as the fountain-head of their inspiration and went out from there to build the great cathedrals of Sens and Noyon, Senlis, Laon, Soissons and Notre Dame in Paris herself – and in the thirteenth century the greatest of all, such masterworks as Chartres (Pl. L), Reims, Amiens (Pl. J), Beauvais and Bourges. One of the supremely important works of the time is the Royal Portal of Chartres, with two towers and a *flèche* and three splendid doorways.

The earliest Gothic interiors, such as Sens, were three-storied as in England, with arcade, gallery and clerestory. Laon (*187*) illustrates a brief phase of four stories, with a triforium added above the gallery and below the clerestory; there, too, all the columns were made the same, the earlier alternation of size giving way to smoother rhythms, a more pronounced horizontality and presently the abandonment of sexpartite vaulting.

Cathedral plans became more clearly articulated in three basic parts: west, centre and east – but hardly any exteriors were really completed. Even Laon's five towers were originally intended to be seven. In the more distant provinces Romanesque plan-types survived. Angers, about 1150, has three enormous cross-vaults, and Poitiers, two decades later, is very similar.

187

SEXPARTITE
VAULT: EACH
PORTION OF
VAULT COVERING
TWO BAYS

GALLERY TRIFORIUM CLERESTORY

ARCADE

NAVE ARCADE
LAON c.1180

EAST AMBULATORY
ST DENIS ABBEY
c.1140

188

L

FRENCH HIGH GOTHIC, 1180 to 1280

By the end of the twelfth century the Gothic style in France was already approaching full maturity. Chartres (*198*), begun about 1195, returned to the system of quadripartite vaults and no gallery; it has tall arcades and clerestory and a low triforium between. Bourges (*197*), begun at the same time illustrates, perhaps better than any other cathedral, the marvellous interplay of structural forces (*182*).

Reims, begun in 1221, has the earliest bar tracery, the beginnings of what in England we call Geometric Decorated. There the piers end at the arch-springing in a broad leaf-capital; at Amiens ten years later many of the shafts soar into a vault 140 feet above the ground (Pl. J).

From now on, the passion for ever higher vaults, ever bigger windows and ever more slender columns and walls was matched by increasing skill and daring and checked only occasionally by disasters. The quire vault of Beauvais, the highest of all at 157 feet (even Westminster Abbey is only 102 feet), exceeded the limit of safety; drastic repairs proved necessary and attempts to extend westwards ended in failure.

At the former cathedral of St Nazaire in Carcassonne, and in some churches of Burgundy, very slender round columns, often without capitals, give an astonishingly brittle appearance. New construction during the period 1250-80, however, mostly followed the precedents set first at Saint Denis and more particularly at Amiens and Beauvais; other magnificent examples, no longer confined to the Île-de-France, are Clermont-Ferrand, Limoges, Narbonne and Rodez. The cathedrals of Normandy remained somewhat akin to English, frequently with specially fine steeples, like that of Coutances.

Rayonnant, the French word for High or Second Gothic, distinguishes its wheel-traceried windows from those of the earlier *Gothique à Lancettes*.

189

QUADRIPARTITE VAULT

CLERESTORY
WINDOW
BEAUVAIS
c. 1240

190

TALL CLERESTORY
WITH SMALL
WALK-WAY BELOW

NO TRIFORIUM

STILTED ARCHES
ROUND APSE

191

INTERIOR OF QUIRE **LE MANS** c. 1220

WEST DOORWAY **SENLIS** c. 1190

FRENCH LATE GOTHIC, 1280 onwards

After 1280 the passion for invention had lost its force. Wars caused the slowing down of building projects, but by then the science of church construction was in any event so mature that architects were largely content to accept and copy their predecessors' methods.

In the latter part of the fourteenth century, however, the more peaceful state of the country encouraged the development of the Flamboyant style. Possibly it was influenced by English curvilinear Decorated, but the degree of elaboration in exaggerated curved patterns of window tracery, in openwork carving and inter-penetrating mouldings, and indeed in enrichment every-where for its own sake, went far beyond anything north of the Channel. The west front of Tours (*192*) is a splen-did example.

Gradually Gothic was sup-planted by Renaissance details: Auch continued to be built in Gothic till 1597, but its west front was finished in 1685 in classical form. Arras cathedral, built in the eighteenth century, is (as one would expect) classical, and yet the towers of Orléans (1790) are in a strange kind of Gothic.

Foremost amongst the fanatical Gothic revivalists and restorers of the nineteenth century was the architect Viollet-le-Duc.

MAIN W. WINDOW TOURS c.1490

192

FRENCH AND ENGLISH CATHEDRALS COMPARED

Whilst England developed the Perpendicular style, France continued longer with the Geometric and elaborated it into Flamboyant. Some of the general characteristics follow.

English Cathedrals Long, low, modest and comfortably spread out. East ends square. Horizontal lines emphasized, outside and in. Walls thick and windows widely spaced, with medium-sized buttresses between. Flying buttresses quite simple. Low, heavy, dignified vaults, quadripartite in 12th c.; lierne vaults common later; fan vaults. Infilling stones of vaults laid parallel, using ridge ribs to cover the serrated junctions. Many fine timber roofs. Richly clustered columns, seldom entirely without capitals. 14th-c. work exuberantly lavish in detail; 15th-c. greatly simplified. Noble rationalization of mouldings in late Gothic; repetitive work, now monotonous after almost universal destruction of glass and statuary in 16th c.

French Cathedrals Shorter, lofty, daring and vigorously pulled together. East ends have chevets with radiating chapels. Soaring verticals dominating the horizontals. Walls thin and windows sometimes so closely spaced as to leave only the buttresses separating them (but windows progressively smaller towards the Mediterranean). Complex tiered flying buttress systems. Extremely lofty, light, simple vaults, sexpartite in 12th c.; no liernes or pendant or fan vaults. *Voutains* (vault infilling stones) tapered and laid with upward bow (each vault panel 'domed'). Purely timber roofs uncommon. Column and arch mouldings weak and often illogical; capitals eventually omitted altogether. 14th-c. work impoverished by Hundred Years' War. 15th-c. often extravagantly elaborate. Bewildering multiplication of shafts in late Gothic. Indescribably beautiful stained glass and profoundly emotional sculpture.

CATHEDRALS OF FRANCE
Brief descriptions of a selection of the greatest:

Albi Languedoc. Immensely strong fortified brick hall-church with five equal aisles (*193*). Outer walls nearly 100 feet high with enormous buttresses and tall thin windows. Contrastingly lavish S. porch of Spanish character. Superb 15th-c. *jubé* and 16th-c. stalls.

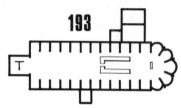

Amiens Picardy. Rebuilt 1220-88 and thus contemporary with Salisbury; with its unified and consistent plan (*194*), high-vaulted interior (Pl. J) and refined structural system, rightly regarded as the epitome of French Gothic. Great portals with superb sculpture.

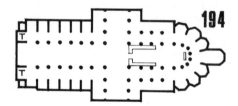

Angoulême Angoumois. Romanesque, mostly of 1105-23. Aisleless Latin-cross plan (*195*) with high central lantern-dome, and smaller domes over nave. W front rich with sculpture (Pl. N).

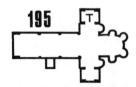

Auch Gascony. Rebuilt 1489-1597, but twin-towered W front late 17th c. 16th-c. quire stalls amongst finest in France. Glass of 1513 and 1648.

Autun Burgundy. 1120-32, Romanesque of the peculiarly Burgundian type with near-classical pilasters and mouldings (*183*) but powerfully carved, immensely varied capitals. Sculpture probably the finest and most famed of its period anywhere in Europe – most sublime of all being the great W portal. 15th-c. central steeple.

Auxerre Champagne. Quire rebuilt in 13th c. and nave in 14th c. Splendid façades to W end and transepts. 16th-c. NW tower. Generous clerestories and ingenious vault systems. Crypt *c.* 1030 with wall-paintings. Much excellent glass and small-scale sculpture.

Bayeux Normandy. W towers, crypt and clustered nave piers and arches Romanesque. Remainder mostly 13th c. Specially beautiful apsed quire. Rich Geometric tracery in both transepts and in upper part of nave. Central lantern 19th c.

Bayonne Gascony. Though remote from Soissons, not unlike it in proportions and Geometric detail. High vaults and dominant flying buttresses. Good glass. W spires added and façade finished in 19th c. 13th-c. cloister (*89*).

Beauvais Île-de-France. Incredibly high 13th-c. quire (156 feet) standing alone; nave hardly commenced (*196*). Interior awe-inspiring in the seemingly impossible height and fragility of its vault and windows (*190*). Flamboyant detail in transepts and outer chapels.

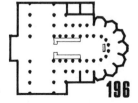

196

Bourges Berry. Mòstly 1199-1230. Five-aisled with crypt under entire building and no transepts at all (*197*). Triforium and clerestory to nave and to each inner aisle (*182*). Five grand W portals. Excellent medieval glass. Berry monument *c.* 1430.

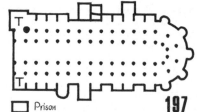

197

□ Prison

Chartres Île-de-France. Late 12th and early 13th c., comparatively massive in construction (*198*). Nave 1194-1220 (the widest in France) but Royal Portal at W end *c.* 1150, renowned for its stylized elongated figures (Pl. L). N. and S transept portals *c.* 1230, devoted to Old and New Testament subjects respectively. Beautifully proportioned SW tower 350 feet high *c.* 1150. Slightly taller, much more elaborate NW tower *c.* 1510. Unfortunate overlay of 18th-c. stonework around apse. Quire screen 1514-17 with scenes of life of Christ. Glass very largely 13th c., probably the finest anywhere in the world: nearly 4000 scenes in 174 windows.

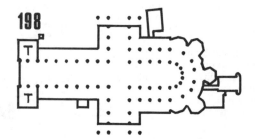

198

Clermont-Ferrand Auvergne. Of fully-developed Île-de-France type and very like Limoges. 1248-1340, but W front 19th c. Splendid chevet and unusually short nave.

Coutances Normandy. Rebuilt 1251-74. Specially notable for its soaring twin W steeples and octagonal central lantern-tower. Well proportioned arcades and beautiful chevet.

Dol Brittany. Unusual plan with big transepts and square-ended quire. Variously 12th to 16th c. Interesting porches.

Evreux Normandy. Diverse in dates and styles through vicissitudes of wars. Nave partly late 11th c. Beautiful quire of *c.* 1275-1340 and even better N transept of Flamboyant design (mid-16th c.) with elaborate façade. Unbalanced W towers with classical detail, not completed till 1609.

Laon Île-de-France. Outstandingly placed on isolated hill in a wide plain. Supreme example of early Gothic, *c.* 1180-1225 (*199*). Four-storied interior with low triforium on top of tall gallery (*187*). Rectangular E end with great rose window. Three deep W portals and unique twin towers with open diagonal buttresses and sculptured bulls.

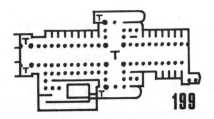

199

Le Mans Maine. Noted for its magnificent soaring quire and chevet, 1217-54 (*189*). Romanesque nave and portals with fine carving. Much early 12th-c. glass. Splendid tapestries, organ case and quire stalls.

Le Puy Languedoc. In the incredible city of volcanic crags and craters. Romanesque, of red, black and white stone. Cruciform, with domes and central lantern and E tower of seven diminishing stages. Black and white cloister also Romanesque.

Limoges Limousin. Rebuilding begun in late 13th c. in style of Île-de-France, much like Clermont-Ferrand. Nave and N transept Flamboyant, not completed till 15th c. Good W tower. Much 14th-c. glass. Elaborate early Renaissance *jubé* now at W end.

Lisieux Normandy. Early Gothic nave finished 1181, with prominent triforium. Quire and chevet early 13th c., modest in height and ornamentation. Two different W towers.

Meaux Île-de-France. Superb late 13th-c. quire and chevet. W parts later. Double-aisled nave of only three bays.

Nantes Brittany. Mostly Flamboyant (rebuilding begun 1434). Height of nave emphasized by tall clerestory and verticality of column mouldings. Very fine early 16th-c. monument to Duke of Brittany.

Narbonne Languedoc. Late 13th-c. quire in Île-de-France style, third in height after Beauvais and Amiens. Nave left unfinished after more than one abortive start.

Noyon Île-de-France. Early Gothic quire finished 1157 and four-storied nave 1220. Large W narthex and two tall towers (the southern 14th c.). Chapter house, cloister and library still remain – rarities in France.

Paris Île-de-France. Always called Notre Dame (*200*). Mostly Early Gothic, 1163-1208. W front 1208-25 and W towers *c.* 1250. Much altered from original design in 13th c.: e.g. double clerestory made into great single windows, chapels added outside aisles, and transepts lengthened. Famous carved demons on W front.

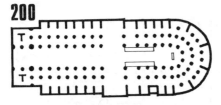

Quimper Brittany. Begun 1234, but almost all Flamboyant. W steeples 1854-6. Marvellous detail in granite.

Reims Champagne. The coronation church of France. Early 13th c., one of the earliest fully developed

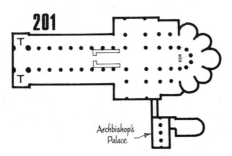

instances of *Rayonnant* or Geometric. Perhaps the finest W front of all, in its architecture and sculpture. Exceptionally spacious nave; quire double-aisled for ceremonial purposes (*201*). Devastated in World War I and faithfully restored.

Rouen Normandy. Mostly of 1202-60 (*202*). Massive NW tower 12th c.; SW 'Butter' tower and much of W front *c.* 1500. Splendid N and S portals. Lady Chapel 1302-20. Central cast-iron spire 512 feet high added in 19th c.

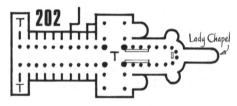

St Denis Abbey Île-de-France. Never a cathedral, but outstandingly important as the principal birthplace of Gothic architecture. Quire (*188*) and W front 1132-44; nave between them rebuilt in High Gothic.

Senlis Île-de-France. Comparatively small. Mostly of 1153-91, with beautiful W portal (*191*). Graceful SW steeple 13th c.

Sens Île-de-France. Early Gothic (12th c.), in internal design the forerunner of Canterbury. Flamboyant transepts with marvellous early 16th-c. rose windows. Much fine glass of various periods.

Soissons Île-de-France. Small and elegant. Apse-ended S transept late 12th c. Remainder *c.* 1210-50; rich SW tower finished in 14th c. Extensively restored after World War I.

Strasbourg Alsace. (*203*) Very short Romanesque apsed quire with tower over crossing. High Gothic nave, *c.* 1250-90. Superb W front with double-traceried windows and single 15th-c. steeple 466 feet high. Exceptional N doorway with triple gable. Unique and incredibly elaborate clock mechanisms of 1352-54 and later.

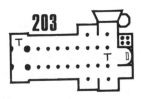

Tours Touraine. Progressively later from east to west, and thus exhibiting the whole history of French Gothic from 13th-c. quire to Flamboyant W front completed 1547 (*192*). Excellent glass.

Other French cathedrals perhaps just short of the first rank include:

Aix-en-Provence	Lyon	Rodez
Angers	Mantes	St Bertrand de
Besançon	Metz	Comminges
Béziers	Moulins	St Omer
Bordeaux	Nevers	St Pol de Léon
Cahors	Orléans	Sées
Châlons-sur-Marne	Perpignan	Tréguier
Langres	Poitiers	

The earliest surviving cathedral buildings date from the time of Charlemagne, about 800. Aachen cathedral (*205*) was, in fact, begun by him as a royal mausoleum; the arcade design and octagonal plan (*208*), entirely Byzantine in character, were derived from the church of St Vitale at Ravenna in Italy, 150 years older still.

The western apse is more or less peculiar to Germany; whether it originated as a baptistry or as a place for the bishop (distinct from the monastic clergy at the east end) is still unknown. Hildesheim cathedral, *c*. 1000, has at *both* ends an apse, a transept and a crossing-tower; like other so-called Ottonian Romanesque (round-arched) churches its plan is based on squares divided into twos and threes, the placing of round and octagonal turrets giving a varied, picturesque skyline. Speyer (*210*) is similar.

Affinities between German and Lombardian Romanesque are traceable to political connections; they include raised quires and external galleries beneath the eaves (*204*). Main vaults often have domical compartments because of the diagonal ribs being semi-circular.

Though Paderborn cathedral had pointed arches as early as 1140, the round-arched style persisted in Germany much longer than elsewhere and indeed right up to the middle of the 13th century. In England and France Gothic evolved from Romanesque; German Gothic, however, took its character direct from the French – much less convincingly in its constructional detail than in its decoration and sculpture.

Clerestories in the earlier German Gothic churches begin almost immediately above the arcades. Hall-churches (*Hallenkirchen*) with nave and aisles of equal height, and enormous roofs over all, were standard practice from about 1350. Many quires were added regardless of an abrupt change of height at the junction (*205*). Chevets of the French type were by no means unknown

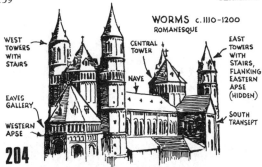

WORMS c. 1110-1200
ROMANESQUE

WEST
TOWERS
WITH
STAIRS

CENTRAL
TOWER

EAST
TOWERS
WITH
STAIRS,
FLANKING
EASTERN
APSE
(HIDDEN)

NAVE

EAVES
GALLERY

WESTERN
APSE

SOUTH
TRANSEPT

204

(Cologne (*209*), Prague, Lübeck). In the north brick was used almost exclusively, even for window tracery. Twin west towers (Regensburg) or gigantic single ones (Freiburg) invariably carry spires, often of openwork tracery (pl. Q). Even spired wooden tabernacles in quires attain heights of as much as 90 feet.

Interpenetrating mouldings (*207*) often make structurally meaningless network patterns (*206*). Flying ribs, double-curved ribs and arches, twisted columns, and columns and mouldings in the form of tree-branches were amongst their other fancies.

German dislike of blank unornamented space is evident in Gothic work – and even more so in the Renaissance. Of the latter little can be said here, for comparatively few cathedrals were built or added to after the Reformation although the south remained largely Catholic. Salzburg in Austria is of 1614-28, a stately building clearly deriving most of its form and detail from Italy. The fantastic stucco and fresco decoration of south German Baroque make the churches look more like gigantic drawing-rooms, but the reconstructed interiors of Freising and Wurzburg are the only major instances amongst cathedrals.

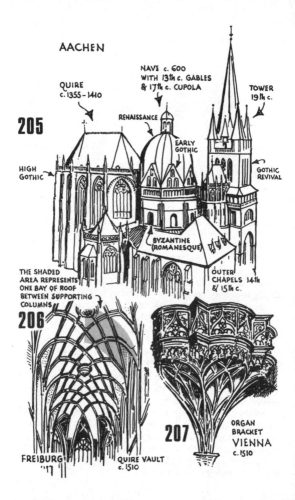

AACHEN

205

QUIRE
c. 1355 - 1440

NAVE c. 600
WITH 13th c. GABLES
& 17th c. CUPOLA

RENAISSANCE

EARLY
GOTHIC

TOWER
19th c.

HIGH
GOTHIC

GOTHIC
REVIVAL

BYZANTINE
(ROMANESQUE)

OUTER
CHAPELS 14th
& 15th c.

THE SHADED
AREA REPRESENTS
ONE BAY OF ROOF
BETWEEN SUPPORTING
COLUMNS

206

FREIBURG
'17

QUIRE VAULT
c. 1510

207

ORGAN
BRACKET
VIENNA
c. 1510

CATHEDRALS OF GERMANY

Brief descriptions of a selection of the greatest:

Aachen (Aix-la-Chapelle) Rhineland (*208*). Domed octagonal nave built as mausoleum by Charlemagne 796-804. Surrounding chapels 14th and 15th c. Tall Gothic quire 1353-1413 (*205*). Tower more recent.

Cologne (Köln) Rhineland. Gothic on gigantic scale (*209*). Begun 1248; work abandoned 1560 and not completed till 1824-80. Vaults 150 feet high and twin steeples 500 feet high, dwarfing rest of building (Pl. Q). Disproportionately short nave and low aisles.

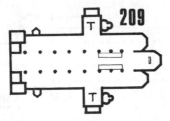

Freiburg in Breisgau Baden. 1122-1252. Quire net-vault of 1510-13 (*206*) derived from that of Prague. Single tower with lace-like spire 385 feet high, completed *c.* 1340. 5-ton bell. Noted altarpiece paintings.

Hildesheim Hanover. Romanesque but with internal Baroque remodelling of *c.* 1720. Superb bronze doors, 1015; font and commemorative column of same date.

Limburg on the Lahn Hesse. Seven-towered, mostly of 1213-42. Romanesque showing transition to Gothic; interior altered in 13th c. to resemble Laon (France). Dominating position above river.

Lübeck Holstein. Romanesque brick, 1173. Gothic quire and aisles 1335.

Mainz (Mayence) Hesse. 11th c., fully developed Romanesque, with large tall central tower. Austere interior. Quire screen *c.* 1330 with fine figure carving.

Regensburg (Ratisbon) Bavaria. 1375-1534. Twin W steeples completed 1869. Delicate little triangular W porch. Cloister of mingled Gothic and Renaissance design.

Speyer (Spires) Palatinate. Many-towered Romanesque (*210*), begun 1030. Mosaics and Corinthian-type capitals due to Italian craftsmen. W end added *c.* 1700 after fire.

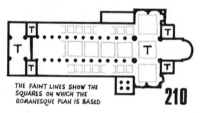

THE FAINT LINES SHOW THE
SQUARES ON WHICH THE
ROMANESQUE PLAN IS BASED

210

Trier (Trèves) Rhineland. 1016-47, with W and E apses. Remains of Roman basilica incorporated. 18th-c. Baroque treasury housing the seamless Robe of Christ.

Worms Hesse. So-called 'Kaiserdom'. Two polygonal towers at each end, flanking apses. Low crossing-tower near E end (*204*). Splendid Baroque altar, 1741.

Other German cathedrals perhaps short of the first rank include:

Augsburg	Eichstatt	Naumburg
Bamberg	Erfurt	Passau
Bremen	Frankfurt	Schleswig
Brunswick	Halberstadt	Wurzburg
Constance	Magdeburg	

The following lie outside Germany:

Cracow Poland. Gothic of 1320-64 but crypt Romanesque. Rectangular quire with 16th-c. Renaissance chapels. Much altered in 18th c. Burial place of Polish kings and heroes.

Prague Czechoslovakia. 14th c. Gothic, built when Prague was capital of the Holy Roman Empire. Quire and chevet of 1344-85, French in style at base and much more fanciful in upper parts. Twin W steeples.

Vienna Austria (St Stephen's). Three-apsed hall-church of 1300-1510 with gigantic roof and magnificent single steeple over S transept (N tower incomplete) (*211*). Net-vault of nave and aisles 1446. Rich pulpit (*207*).

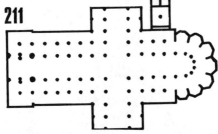

211

In Switzerland Basel and Lausanne deserve mention; in Austria: Salzburg; in Czechoslovakia: Bratislava, Košice (Kassa).

The churches of Belgium reflect the character of those of neighbouring Germany or France, according to their nearness. Good stone and timber have always been plentiful; the famous black marble of Tournai was even exported to England in some quantity in Norman times (the font at Winchester is made of it).

Dutch exteriors are typically of warm red brick, often slightly leaning, mirrored in the deep dark waters of canals and hemmed in by small dwellings hugging their great buttresses (214). Successive repairs over the centuries have deprived them of their carved detail, leaving them rich in texture and colour but shapeless in outline. In the northern part of the country especially, the few former cathedrals are used by Protestants (the 'Re-

ANTWERP
1352 – 1592

213

N·W TOWER
1422 – 1518

CENTRAL 'ONION'
SPIRE FROM SPANISH
OCCUPATION c.1550

UNFINISHED
S·W TOWER

NAVE
ROOF

N·TRANSEPT

S·AISLE
ROOFS

QUIRE
BEGUN
1521

S·TRANSEPT

formed Church') who in reordering the interiors have shifted the focus from altar to pulpit, whitewashed the walls and in many instances installed splendid organs.

Both countries have been coveted by other powers over the centuries; the bulbous or 'onion' domes sometimes met with are reminders of the Spanish occupation (*213*). Carillons of bells are another distinctive feature: the finest is at Tournai.

CATHEDRALS OF THE LOW COUNTRIES
Brief descriptions of a selection of the greatest:

Antwerp Belgium. Begun 1352, mostly in Flamboyant style (*212, 213*). W front with richly pinnacled 402-foot NW steeple, begun 1422; SW tower incomplete. Quire 1518-92. Nave 130 feet high, flanked by much lower aisles. Rubens' 'Descent from the Cross' in S transept; two other Rubens pictures and many by other masters. Carillon of 47 bells.

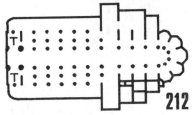

212

Gent Belgium. Quire 13th-14th c. Tower 1462-1534. Nave and transepts not completed till 1559. Splendid oak and marble pulpit 1745. Many paintings, including van Eyck's 'Adoration of the Lamb'.

Haarlem Holland. Now the Protestant *Groote Kerk*. Begun late in 14th c. and consecrated 1519. Wooden vault 141 feet high. Tower 262 feet high. Fine brass screen 1509-17. Very famous organ of 1735-8.

Malines Belgium. Metropolitan cathedral of Belgium, almost all 15th c. 325-foot tower.

Tournai Belgium. Five-towered Romanesque, largely of black marble, proud and challenging. 435 feet long. Nave, central lantern-tower and apse-ended transepts.

Other cathedrals perhaps just short of the first rank include:

Belgium: Bruges   Holland: Dordrecht
        Liège   s'Hertogenbosch
        Mons   Maastricht
                             Utrecht (Protestant)

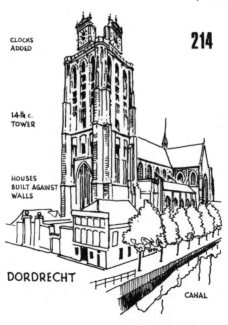

CLOCKS ADDED

214

14-th c. TOWER

HOUSES BUILT AGAINST WALLS

DORDRECHT

CANAL

South of the Alps Gothic architecture never gained a firm foothold, for the classical tradition was too strong. Ancient Roman forms continued in use in Italy right up to the fourteenth and fifteenth centuries, when they began to be scientifically studied.

The earliest greater churches were basilicas, a type of building with long nave and single or double aisles which served equally well as a market hall or a law-court. At one end was usually an apse or semi-circular termination, and at the other a narthex or portico. If it was to be a cathedral the bishop's throne was placed in the apse behind the stone altar, and the priests' desks in the quarter-circles on each side of it. An example is the cathedral of St John Lateran, Rome (224), later largely reconstructed. Later on, it became the practice to house a saint's shrine in a crypt under the altar, with a *confessio* or opening to make it visible from the nave.

In the fifth and sixth centuries, Ravenna became pre-eminent as a trading port. Ravennate churches, like the cathedral of Parenzo (now Poreč, Yugoslavia), have Byzantine details, most striking being the pulvins or impost blocks above the column capitals, and the formalized carvings of foliage, birds and animals.

Italian Romanesque is distinguished even more than that of other countries by the extensive use of wall-arcades, often tier upon tier (Pl. K, P). Many basilicas were improved in the eleventh and twelfth centuries, and new churches built in similar form. Often, as at Lucca, the details were still almost classical in their refinement. Large baptistries (another peculiarly Italian feature) were added, as at Cremona (217), and polygonal cupolas over crossings, as at Parma. Tall *campanili* or bell-towers became frequent. Mosaic decoration, often by the so-called Cosmati workers or by Venetians, was especially popular at this period.

SIENA (GOTHIC)
W· FRONT LATE 13TH C. AT BASE
& LATE 14TH C. IN UPPER PARTS

215

NAVE &
DOME
EARLY
14TH C.

CAMPANILE
13TH C.

(EARLY AND LATER
ROMANESQUE)

217

216

S·AISLE TORCELLO c.1010

BAPTISTRY
CREMONA 1167

Sicily and the provinces of Apulia and Calabria have Norman cathedrals with pointed arches due to Moorish, not Gothic, influence (Cefalù is an example).

The cathedral of Milan (222) is the greatest Gothic building of Italy. But its lavish sculptural detail hides a curious lack of appreciation of the vault-and-buttress system which the French had mastered so thoroughly. More typically Italian is Siena (215), with round-headed main arcades but a later pointed clerestory, ornate W front, ambitious hexagonal central cupola and tall campanile, and richly banded black and white marble facings inside and out. The classical 'survival' is still evident in the general shapes of wall-piers and cornices.

The classical 'revival' began in Italy in the fifteenth century. Brunelleschi was the first real architect of the style, his inventiveness making possible the construction of the great octagonal dome of Florence (1420) (221). The work of Alberti and Bramante may be studied at Rimini (1450) (218) and Pavia (1488) and it is not hard to see how the architecture of all three was to influence that of Wren two centuries afterwards (76).

Michelangelo (1475-1564), carried on the work of Bramante and, more than anyone else, was responsible for the unequalled splendour of St Peter's at Rome.

The style called Baroque originated in the sixteenth century. Its characteristics are flowing or even con-torted lines and a striving after the picturesque. Bernini created the gorgeous baldacchino of St Peter's and the colonnades which enclose its main front. His successor Borromini remodelled the interior of St John Lateran (220). The Spanish domination of the south fostered some distinctive Baroque, as at Amalfi and Lecce.

By the eighteenth century the ingenuity of designers seemed largely spent; fine façades like Syracuse (219) are less common than impersonal conceptions such as Ravenna. Too often, also, ancient churches were altered and their real age completely disguised.

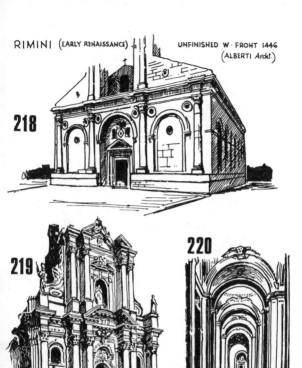

RIMINI (EARLY RENAISSANCE) UNFINISHED W·FRONT 1446
(ALBERTI Archt.)

218

219

220

SYRACUSE (BAROQUE)
W·FRONT 1728-54 (PALMA Archt.)

ROME ST JOHN (BAROQUE)
LATERAN
N·AISLE OF NAVE c.1650
(BORROMINI Archt.)

CATHEDRALS OF ITALY

Brief descriptions of a selection of the greatest:

Amalfi Salernitano. Basilica of *c.* 1200, internally embellished in Baroque style of 1701-31. Gilded ceiling with painted panels. Cloister of Paradise under Moorish influence, 1266. Set in a rocky coastal city.

Cefalù Sicily. A blend of Romanesque and Moorish, *c.* 1140. Low two-towered nave and much taller E end. Byzantine mosaics, those at the E end unsurpassed.

Ferrara Lombardy. Rich early Gothic façades of 12th and 13th c. Interior grandiosely reconstructed *c.* 1720.

Florence (Firenze) Tuscany. Domed cruciform, a marvellously harmonious blend of Gothic and early Renaissance (*221*). Begun 1296 but not complete till 1588; W front 1887. Interior plain and noble; exterior multi-coloured and complex. Magnificent central cupola 140 feet in diameter by Brunelleschi, 1420. Campanile begun by Giotto 1334. Separate baptistry probably of 5th and 11th c. with celebrated bronze doors of 1330.

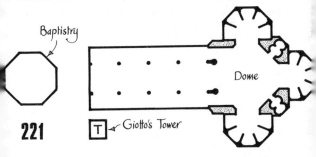

221

Messina Sicily. Very severely damaged by earthquake in 1908 and by war in 1943, but restored. Romanesque under Norman and Moorish influences.

Milan Lombardy. (*222*) The largest of all medieval cathedrals except Seville (*239*). Begun *c.* 1385 but not finished till *c.* 1810. Mostly Gothic, peculiarly Italian in its proportions and horizontality. Enormous over-heavy canopied column-capitals. 15th-c. main vault 148 feet high. Central lantern 1490 with spire of 1750. W front largely classical, begun 1653. Glass of E windows 15th and 16th c. Rich quire stalls, baldacchino and bronze pulpits *c.* 1600.

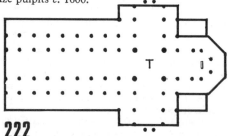

222

Modena Lombardy. Romanesque, 1099-1184. Architecturally important for its completeness and its early figure carving on internal capitals and on W front. Vaults added later. 13th-c. campanile 300 feet high.

Monreale Sicily. Stately Norman, late 12th c. Incomplete two-towered W front. Three-apsed E end strongly ornamented with wall-arcading. Broad nave with pointed arches on re-used classical granite columns. Magnificent contemporary glass mosaics throughout. Patterned presbytery floor. Bronze W doors 1186. Cloister with unusually rich figure-carving.

Orvieto Tuscany. Romanesque in basilican form, begun *c.* 1290. Little apsidal chapels along aisle walls. Vaulted crossing and transepts Gothic, *c.* 1320. W front begun at same time, splendidly proportioned and beautifully carved. Superb quire stalls *c.* 1330.

Palermo Sicily. Norman coronation church of kingdom of Sicily, begun 1185. Internally transformed by Fuga 1781; nave shortened and central dome added. Moorish-Gothic S porch early 15th c. Magnificent royal tombs.

Parma Lombardy. Comparatively short yet grand and complete example of Romanesque. Campanile c. 1290. Aisle chapels later. Splendid paintings throughout walls and vaults 16th c. Detached early 16th-c. baptistry.

Pavia Lombardy. Renaissance Greek Cross plan. Begun 1487 under influence of Bramante and still not absolutely complete. Original wooden model largely adhered to through the centuries and still preserved. Main apse completed 1507 but quire not vaulted till 17th c. Central dome finished 1885. Transept apses only begun 1930.

Pisa Tuscany. Romanesque double-aisled basilica with addition of transepts and lengthened presbytery (*223*, Pl. P). Begun c. 1089. Richly arcaded externally. Ancient classical columns re-used throughout. Unusual elliptical dome. Pulpit c. 1310. Campanile (the 'Leaning Tower') 1174-1350, now 14 feet out of vertical. Circular baptistry 1153-c. 1400 with conical roof projecting through dome.

223

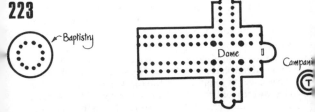

Ravenna Veneto. Rebuilt c. 1740 in uninspired late Renaissance style. Round campanile 10th c. Detached octagonal vaulted baptistry mid-5th c., with remarkable mosaics and plaster reliefs.

Rome (St John Lateran). Known as the Mother of Churches and the Cathedral of the World (*224*). Originally a double-aisled basilica of *c.* 320. Transepts probably 9th c., transformed in Renaissance style *c.* 1600. Nave and aisles similarly altered by Borromini (*220*). E apse extended in 19th c. 'Cosmatesque' cloister *c.* 1220.

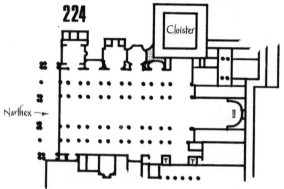

St Peter's at Rome, the largest church in the world, is not a cathedral but the church of the Papal *Curia* in the Vatican. 1506-1614, largely by Michelangelo.

Siena Tuscany. Largely 13th-c. Romanesque but E end rebuilt in Gothic style, and nave, clerestory and vault added early in 14th c. Hexagonal central dome. New nave, at right angles to old, begun in 14th c. but abandoned; old façades then completed (*215*). Banded exterior and graceful campanile. Interior rich with gold and deep blue in vaults and inlaid marble in pavements. Pulpit 1265.

Syracuse Sicily. Originally the Greek temple of Athena, *c.* 480 B.C. and thus the oldest church building in existence. Converted into a cathedral in 7th c. W front *c.* 1730 (*219*).

Torcello Veneto. Aisled basilica of 1008 (*216*), preserving not only 7th-c. building plan but also archaic position of bishop's throne in apse behind altar. Island-village site.

Venice Veneto. Always known as St Mark's. Originally the Doge's Palace Chapel, rebuilt 1063-94. Chiefly Byzantine as a result of trading links with eastern Mediterranean, unlike other Italian cathedrals (*225*). *Matroneum* or low gallery around each arm of cross. Rich and extensive mosaics and sculpture, including innumerable works brought by merchants from overseas. Campanile 323 feet high, focal point of Piazza and Piazzetta.

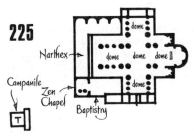

Other Italian cathedrals perhaps just short of the first rank include:

Albenga	Genoa	Rimini
Aquileia	Grado	Salerno
Assisi	Lecce	Spoleto
Bari	Lucca	Trani
Bologna	Molfetta	Troia
Civita Castellana	Noto	Turin
Como	Piacenza	Tuscania
	Ravello	

The cathedrals of Spain owe their special qualities to
a constant flow of artistic influences from abroad (chiefly
from France and Morocco but also to some extent from
Italy, Germany and even England), to several distinctive plan features, and perhaps most of all to the fact
that their treasures have never suffered wholesale
destruction or pillaging at the hands of reformers.

Although not monastic, most cathedrals have chapter
houses and cloisters. The gradual adding of chapels,
sacristies and other buildings has in many cases obscured
the external form of the main structure, which is usually
rather wider and lower than its French equivalent.
Orientation has never mattered much in Spain: few
cathedrals face true east. The most unusual – to English
eyes very odd – feature, however, is the *coro* or choir
enclosure within the nave, approached by a screened
passage from the presbytery (229). It obviated the need
for an eastward extension to provide a dignified setting
for enlarged choirs, but detracts from the internal grandeur and seriously restricts the congregational space.

The Moors attacked Spain early in the eighth century
and Christianity soon became confined to a narrow strip
in the north. However, Christian kingdoms were later
founded one by one in the freed areas, until eventually
Seville and Córdoba were won back early in the thirteenth century. During the Dark Ages the Moorish (or
Islamic or Saracenic) culture of southern Spain was the
most advanced in Europe, and some cathedrals retain
traces of it. Seville's enormous plan (239), for instance,
is largely that of the great mosque which preceded it,
and its minaret, the beautiful *Giralda* of 1184-98, still
stands (228). At Córdoba the former mosque (*la
Mezquita*) actually contains the cathedral (226).

Historians cannot be sure whether the Gothic ribbed
vault and pointed arch owe anything to their Moorish

HORSESHOE ARCHES
CORDOBA
c.970

226

CENTRAL LANTERN.

TRANSEPT GABLE

EAVES GALLERY

227

ROMANESQUE

S. TRANSEPT APSE **SEO DE URGEL**
c.1140

ARCH OF NEW CATHEDRAL
↑ c.1530

MOORISH

ROMAN COLUMNS RE-USED

DOORWAY TO BALCONY
IN MINARET **SEVILLE**
c.1160

28

229

CORO (CHOIR ENCLOSURE)
IN NAVE **SALAMANCA**

NAVE c.1530   CORO c.1730

EAST

S·AISLE

HIGH GOTHIC
UNDER FRENCH
INFLUENCE **230**

VAULT

CLERESTORY

GLAZED
TRIFORIUM

ARCADE

QUIRE ARCADE
LEON c.1260

CENTRAL
LANTERN
TOWER
BURGOS
c.1540

LATE
GOTHIC
231

UPPER PART OF
W· FRONT
SANTIAGO
DE COMPOSTELA
c.1740

RENAISSANCE
(BAROQUE)
232

antecedents. What is certain is that the great pilgrimage route to Santiago de Compostela in the extreme north-west led to great interchanges of culture. The Romanesque style with round arches came from Lombardy, Burgundy and southern France to places like la Seo de Urgel (*227*), Orense and Salamanca. Cathedrals generally had three parallel apses or, exceptionally, a chevet of French type, as at Santiago itself (*238*). The transition to Gothic was marked, as elsewhere, by pointed arches on great clustered piers, as at Tarragona.

Spanish High Gothic was an outcome of the more settled conditions following Christian expansion southward. In its purest, thirteenth-century form (as at Léon, *230*) it is completely French in character. Yet it was probably English masons who introduced lierne vaulting, curvilinear tracery and gargoyles in the fourteenth century, and Germans certainly designed the openwork spires of Burgos (*231*), fifteenth century.

Eastern Spain has several outstanding, more typically Spanish cathedrals of the fourteenth century, notably Barcelona (*233*) with its tall aisles and chevet, and Palma (*237*) whose aisles alone are taller than any English nave and whose nave is taller even than Amiens. The full richness of later Gothic is emphasized more than anywhere else in Europe by contrasts of delicacy with grandeur – the marvellous south porch of Palma framed by immense sword-like buttresses, the incredibly rich *retablo* or reredos amongst the cross-vistas of powerful columns at Seville, and the great pinnacled tower of Toledo rising gaily storey by storey from an austere base.

A similar nobility of scale and proportion distinguishes early Spanish Renaissance cathedrals. The style was assimilated remarkably early (Jaén (*235*) was begun in 1540), yet purely Gothic vaults and buttresses continued to be included as at Guadix. In the seventeenth and eighteenth centuries many wonderfully rich Baroque additions were made, as at Murcia and Santiago (*232*).

CATHEDRALS OF SPAIN

Brief descriptions of a selection of the greatest:

Astorga, Léon. Unusually late Gothic, begun 1471. Nave with four-centred arches like English Tudor, *c.* 1530. Baroque W front and tower, *c.* 1700.

Avila Old Castile. Grey and bastion-like in a grim walled city. Mostly Transitional or early Gothic, 12th and 13th c. Chevet built over city wall, with double aisles, and chapels within wall thickness. Fine cloisters. Rich wrought iron pulpit.

Barcelona Catalonia. 14th c., large, dark and mysterious (*233*). Deep buttresses with chapels between, all round, as at Albi in France, and countless splendid altarpieces. Crypt under high altar with *confessio* of Italian type. 15th-c. cloister, also with chapels. W front 1890-2.

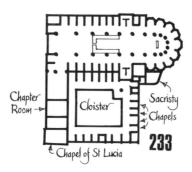

Burgos Old Castile. Begun *c.* 1230 but overlaid with later additions (*234*), culminating in sumptuous central lantern of 1567 (*231*). Twin openwork W spires of German character. Unusually large and elaborate side

chapels, especially St Anna's and the remarkable
eastern Constable's Chapel. Many complex vaults.

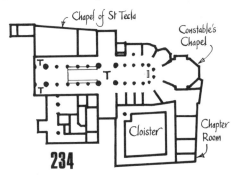

Córdoba Andalusia. Late Gothic, inserted into the
centre of a great Moorish mosque in the 16th c. Dome
and tower of 1600. Extensive horseshoe-arched aisles of
8th- to 10th-c. mosque remain as circulation area
around cathedral, and contain over 800 ancient Roman
and similar columns (*226*). Great Courtyard of Oranges
on N side.

Gerona Catalonia. Early 14th c. E end with chevet.
15th-c. nave, as broad as quire and aisles combined;
at 73 feet, the widest Gothic vault-span in Europe.
Baroque W front *c.* 1730. Romanesque N tower 11th
c., and cloister 12th c. 14th-c. silver altarpiece and
canopy.

Granada Andalusia. Renaissance with Gothic vaults
and other detail; begun 1523, finished 1703. Enormous
five-aisled plan with chapels in outer walls. Clumsy
dome on tall piers, in place of true apse. Baroque W
front. Beautiful late Gothic Royal Chapel adjoining
S side.

Jaén Andalusia. Begun in Gothic style 1512 but re-designed as Renaissance hall-church 1534 (*235*). Not completed till 1726. Outstandingly well-proportioned.

235 Chapter House ⌐

Léon Léon. One of the most perfect and complete of all Gothic buildings, but modest in size and almost purely French in style. Begun *c.* 1260 but S tower not finished till 1472, and last vaulting of cloister only in 1540. Especially beautiful internal design of nave arcades, open triforium and tall clerestory (*230*). Glass of 13th to 16th c. more fully preserved (though restored) than in any other medieval church. Rich 15th-c. stalls.

Lérida Catalonia. Renaissance new cathedral 1764-90. Old cathedral on hill-top restored after two centuries of use as barracks. Transitional and early Gothic, 1203-78 (*236*). 13th- and 14th-c. cloister exceptional both in size and in its western position. 14th-c. octagonal tower.

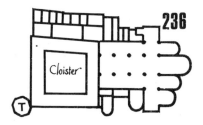

236

Oviedo Asturias. Late Gothic: E end late 14th c., nave late 15th c., the only instance of French Flamboyant style in Spain. Single open-spired tower. Early 9th-c. *camara santa* incorporated into cathedral.

Palma Mallorca. One of the greatest of all medieval cathedrals, for its sea-front site, and for its dramatic structural system enclosing a vast space on very tall slender octagonal columns (*237*). Mostly of 1306-27, but fine S porch *c.* 1400. Main vault 141 feet high. No triforium. Earlier tower on N side. 20th-c. altar canopy by Gaudi.

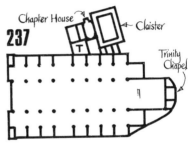

Pamplona Navarre. Mainly 14th c. Unusual chevet combining ambulatory with chapels under a single series of vaults. Splendid cloister *c.* 1500. W front *c.* 1780. Fine sculpture, including tomb of Charles III.

Plasencia Estremadura. In an arrested state of development; rebuilding on extremely grand scale carried on through 16th c. but left with only E parts built. In proportions and detail the culmination of Spanish Gothic; vault-ribs merging into columns and spanning the equal of the entire width of the old nave, and aisles left standing to the west. Square 13th-c. chapter-house with octagonal vault; old cloister also retained.

Salamanca Léon. Old and new cathedrals abutting one another, principal ornaments of a great university city. Smaller one late 12th c. Transitional, famous for circular dome with short octagonal steeple on top. Grand new cathedral begun 1509; heavy clustered piers and star vaults; exterior rich with pinnacles and fine doorways. Magnificent 18th-c. *coro* (*229*).

Santiago de Compostela Galicia. One of the greatest of all pilgrimage centres, housing the shrine of St James the Apostle; in the later Middle Ages a principal re-cipient of colonial wealth (*238*). Romanesque, 1075–1128, with no clerestory, but tall tribune or gallery round whole church. Exterior entirely clothed by Renaissance façades including rich, wide Baroque W front of 1738–50 (*232*). Large cloister of 1521–90, Gothic and classical.

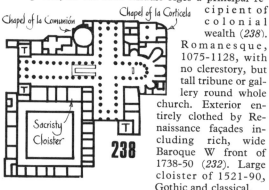

Chapel of la Comunión · Chapel of la Corticela

Sacristy Cloister

238

Saragossa Aragon. Two co-cathedrals: *La Seo* a hall-church on very ancient foundations, successively en-larged and now largely 16th c., with crossing-lantern of rather Moorish character and curious brick tower of c. 1690; *El Pilar* a great Renaissance building begun 1677 but mostly mid-18th c.

Segovia Old Castile. Perhaps the last great Gothic building of all, mostly of 1525–58 (Pl. O). Beautiful late 14th-c. cloister moved to new site when 50 years old. Chevet 1563–91. 289-foot tower completed c. 1620.

Seville Andalusia. *(239)* The largest church in the world, except St Peter's, Rome; on site of mosque and retaining its beautiful minaret (the *Giralda (228)*) and northern Courtyard of Oranges. Begun 1402; completed in Gothic style by 1506 except eastern domed Chapel Royal of 1551-75. Magnificent 16th-c. sacristy and chapter house. Rich stalls and innumerable altarpieces.

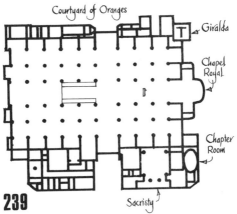

239

Siguenza New Castile. Twin-towered, fortress-like. Basically 12th c., with many later changes. Cloister, chapter house and sacristy 16th c.

Tarragona Catalonia. Transitional on grand scale, begun 1171. Early Gothic cloister.

Toledo New Castile. Outstandingly impressive, inside and out. Five-aisled, rather like Bourges in France *(240)*. Begun 1227; mostly complete by 1493. Grand W front, flanked by superb NW tower of 1425-52 and SW cupola of 1626-31 by son of El Greco. Chapel of Santiago in chevet 1435. Rich *transparente* or reredos of 1752.

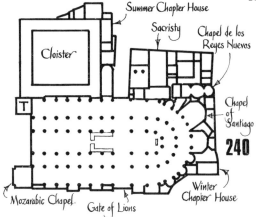

Valencia Valencia. Begun 1262, showing French influence but with unusually low vaults and wide arches; interior remodelled in classical style 1774-9. Central lantern 14th c., with alabaster panels instead of glass. Tall octagonal belfry (*Miguelete*). Baroque W front and transept fronts. Reputed Holy Grail in former chapter house.

Valladolid Old Castile. Gigantic, classical, grey and forbidding. Begun *c.* 1580 and barely half finished.

Other Spanish cathedrals perhaps just short of the first rank include:

Burgo de Osma	Lugo	Seo de Úrgel
Cadiz	Málaga	Tarazona
Ciudad Rodrigo	Murcia	Tortosa
Coria	Orense	Tuy
Cuenca	Orihuela	Vich
Huesca	Palencia	Zamora
Jaca	Santo Domingo de la Calzada	

Until about 1500 architecture in Portugal followed much the same course as in Spain, but none of her cathedrals is outstanding. Good Romanesque work (twelfth century) on a modest scale can be seen at Braga, Porto and particularly at the *Sé Velha* or Old Cathedral of Coimbra. Gothic is best represented by the great monasteries of Alcobaça and Batalha.

The influx of overseas wealth that followed the explorations of Vasco da Gama and other navigators prompted the development of the distinctive Manueline style. This, too, is best seen in the monasteries, especially at Belem and Tomar; Viseu and some other cathedrals contain less important examples. Knotted cables, chains, anchors and sails were used decoratively, sometimes in fantastic compositions bearing no resemblance to any other architectural style.

Renaissance buildings are often rich in unrestrained Baroque carving of doorways and windows, ceilings and altarpieces. Some, like the quire of Evora (1718-46), were inspired by the ornate interiors of Bavaria. Many minor cathedrals like Aveiro (*241*) are older structures dressed up with classical detail. *Azulejos*, distinctively Portuguese blue glazed ornamental tiles, were used inside and out.

AVEIRO 17th c. W. FRONT

The following cathedrals are of special interest, though not of first importance:
Braga
Coimbra (Old and
   New)
Evora
Lisbon   Portalegre
Porto   Viseu

187

The old churches of Norway, Sweden and Denmark are Lutheran; yet in their looks and way of use they retain slightly more of their former Roman Catholic feeling than those of other Protestant countries. Architecturally the cathedrals are undistinguished, the three most important, Lund, Uppsala and Trondhjem (244), being respectively German, French and English in character. North German forms and details are of course the commonest, particularly in Denmark, and the nineteenth-century mania for restoration all too often involved the well-intentioned building of Teutonic gabled and spired tower-tops (as at Aarhus) in place of less correct but picturesque lanterns and cupolas added in the seventeenth and eighteenth centuries.

In Denmark the staple materials are granite and rich red brick, in Sweden stone and wood with some brick, and in Norway mostly wood; the so-called 'stave' churches of Norway are justly famous, but her cathedrals are of course of stone. The use of brick in Denmark and Sweden imposed a drastic simplification of Gothic forms; windows, for instance, never really progressed much beyond lancets and simple uncusped tracery, like those at Odense. The earlier Romanesque work is often quite rich, as at Lund in Sweden.

In all but the greatest churches east ends are generally square. Hall-churches of German type, with nave

242 RIBE
DENMARK

and aisles of equal height, are the most usual; where clerestories exist they are weak in design, and imitative painting (as at Uppsala) has in some cases been used to improve an equally undeveloped triforium. Vaults are usually poor in design and clumsy in execution and where more elaborate forms have been attempted, as at Strängnäs in Sweden, they lack conviction and skill.

The following are the most important cathedrals:

Linköping Sweden. 13th- and 14th-c. grey limestone vaulted hall-church with short quire and chevet. Poor 19th-c. steeple. Good stone carving. Bronze font.

Lund Sweden. Noble early 12th c. Romanesque, an archbishop's seat from 1103 to 1536. Twin grey towers. Nave arcades with paired arches and quadripartite vaults. Extensive crypt under transepts and E apse, with richly carved columns.

Odense Denmark. Founded by Canute 1080. Dignified

CRYPT ODENSE DENMARK   COLUMNS c.1080   VAULTS 14th c.?

red brick with W tower, all except crypt (*243*) now mostly 14th c. Good stalls and 15th-c. reredos.

Ribe Denmark. Grand Romanesque (*242*). Arcades on massive granite piers; triforium gallery over aisles; sexpartite nave vault with addition of ridge ribs. Dissimilar W towers. Good pulpit, stalls and organ case.

Röskilde Denmark. Seat of primate and burial place of kings. Transitional Gothic, begun early in 13th c.; many later chapels; old sanctuary made into royal mausoleum 1689. Simple brick twin W towers. Stalls of 1420. 17th-c. altarpiece. Good organ. Medieval wall-paintings.

Strängnäs Sweden. Spacious 13th c., much altered and rebuilt. Nearly all brick. W tower. Apsidal E end.

Trondhjem Norway. Formerly called Nidaros. Coronation church, begun 1161; Romanesque and early Gothic of English character (*244*). Early 14th-c. octagonal E corona separated from quire by open stone screen. Much restored.

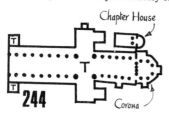

Uppsala Sweden. Archbishop's seat. Begun early in 13th c., perhaps with French architect. Not complete till 1435. Mostly brick, with high spacious interior. Twin W spires. Much spoilt by 18th-c. additions and 19th-c. restoration, and now modern-looking. Royal and other monuments.

Others of interest are at:

Denmark: Aarhus, Maribo, Viborg
Norway: Stavanger
Sweden: Vesteras, Vexio

The fundamental differences between the Western churches and the Eastern (see p. 9) arose from the question whether the Holy Spirit proceeded from the Father and Son (Western) or from the Father only (Eastern). The Emperor Constantine established Christianity in Byzantium (now Istanbul) in 323. His successor Leo III (c. 740) decreed that three-dimensional statues and representations were to be forbidden; thenceforth all ornament was flat and large uninterrupted areas were provided for paintings and mosaics.

Roofs of Byzantine churches are formed as a series of domes, quite unlike the vaulting systems of Gothic. Arches are without mouldings and seldom fulfil a major structural role. Windows are small. Bell-towers do not form part of designs, though when the Moslems turned churches and cathedrals into mosques (e.g. St Sophia at Istanbul) they usually added a minaret. The bulbous domes of Russia (245) were derived from Tartar origins.

The sanctuary in Eastern churches is completely screened off by what in Greece is called the *iconostasis*, usually containing three doors.

The system of bishops and dioceses is much less clearly defined in Eastern Europe. In Russia the largest church in a town of any size is likely to be called a cathedral and to have been one at some time in its history. Further west, there is no hard-and-fast dividing line between Eastern and Byzantine (225) on the one hand and Early Christian (224) and Romanesque on the other. In Yugoslavia, for instance, are examples of both kinds, as well as the extraordinary cathedral of Split which was actually a circular Roman mausoleum. In Greece, at Andravidha, there is even the ruin of a small Gothic cathedral. Poland, Hungary and Rumania have Armenian cathedrals (as at Lwow), Greek Orthodox (as at Cernauti), and Roman Catholic (as at Esztergom).

St Basil's: Yellow
reen & Red

Southern (out of sight):
Orange & White

ST BASIL'S CATHEDRAL · MOSCOW : c.1550

245

OLOURING OF
UPOLAS EARLY
th CENTURY :

Eastern:
Yellow &
Green

NE:
Red & Green:
other corner
cupolas yellow
& green

Northern:
Light Blue
& White

Western:
Dark Red
& Green

Nothing has so far been said about cathedrals outside Europe. Of the many hundreds, a great many are of exceptional architectural interest. Historically the largest and most important group are the Roman Catholic cathedrals established by the Spanish and Portuguese colonists from the sixteenth century onwards, particularly in what is now Latin America, but also in African countries like Angola and Mozambique. Many are like the Spanish cathedral of Jaén, long low early Renaissance buildings with straightforward classical detail: Cuzco in Peru, Merida in Mexico and Léon in Nicaragua are examples. These Spanish-speaking countries later developed their own kinds of Baroque, absorbing the indigenous cultures to a greater or lesser degree, as at Zacatecas in Mexico and Cajamarca in Peru.

In many parts of the world, particularly in the nineteenth century, the Gothic style was held to be the only one possible for religious buildings. Amongst the best known are Washington in the U.S.A., designed by the English architect Bodley, Albany Cathedral (1883) and St Patrick's Cathedral, New York (1850-79), and the Anglican cathedrals at Jerusalem, at Melbourne, Australia and Wellington, New Zealand. Baltimore, also in the U.S.A., is classical (1805-21).

This brief note on overseas buildings would be incomplete without mention of Brasilia, the newly established capital city of Brazil, where Oscar Niemeyer's revolutionary (but unfinished) cathedral is formed of a series of giant boomerang-shaped concrete piers arranged in a circle, not unlike the Roman Catholic cathedral of Liverpool (85).

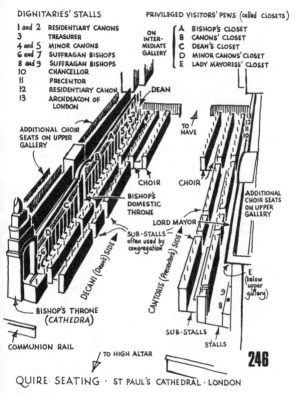

DIGNITARIES' STALLS

1 and 2	RESIDENTIARY CANONS
3	TREASURER
4 and 5	MINOR CANONS
6 and 7	SUFFRAGAN BISHOPS
8 and 9	SUFFRAGAN BISHOPS
10	CHANCELLOR
11	PRECENTOR
12	RESIDENTIARY CANON
13	ARCHDEACON OF LONDON

PRIVILEGED VISITORS' PEWS (called CLOSETS)

ON INTER-MEDIATE GALLERY

A	BISHOP'S CLOSET
B	CANONS' CLOSET
C	DEAN'S CLOSET
D	MINOR CANONS' CLOSET
E	LADY MAYORESS' CLOSET

DEAN

ADDITIONAL CHOIR SEATS ON UPPER GALLERY

TO NAVE

CHOIR   CHOIR

ADDITIONAL CHOIR SEATS ON UPPER GALLERY

BISHOP'S DOMESTIC THRONE

LORD MAYOR

SUB-STALLS often used by congregation

DECANI (Dean's) SIDE

CANTORIS (Precentor's) SIDE

E (below upper gallery)

BISHOP'S THRONE (CATHEDRA)

COMMUNION RAIL

SUB-STALLS   STALLS

246

→ TO HIGH ALTAR

QUIRE SEATING · ST PAUL'S CATHEDRAL · LONDON

NOTE : SEATS ARE NOT NECESSARILY USED EXACTLY AS ALLOCATED
STALLS NOT OTHERWISE INDICATED ARE MOSTLY ASSIGNED TO PREBENDARIES

Greater nowadays than the problems of new cathedral building are those of conservation of the older fabrics, largely from dangers that have arisen in our own age.

Traffic vibration does great harm to fragile stonework, particularly where the joints are of soft mortar and the cores of walls filled with loose material. Bombing and shelling in the two world wars caused incalculable damage in England, France and Germany, and now supersonic aircraft booms are capable of dislodging stonework, plaster and ancient glass. Fumes both from traffic and chimneys cause stain and decay to stonework, especially in cities, and the rusting of tie-bars and other embedded ironwork can cause stones to split. Disastrous subsidence of foundations can be brought about by changes in natural water levels as a result of new building in the vicinity.

If the effects of rain and hail, snow, lightning and gales are added – effects which were known and to some extent allowed for by the builders – as well as the day-to-day deterioration, the wearing of floors, the constant thermal expansion and contraction of lead, the accidental breakage of windows, the fading of fabrics, the ageing of joinery, the ravages of death-watch beetle and dry-rot, it will be seen that the hazards are really formidable.

In every single cathedral a constant watch has to be kept to try to ensure that nothing becomes decayed to the extent where repair becomes impossible or where some other part may become affected as a result.

Maintenance is costly, and the greater cathedrals have their own works staff continually employed. Contrary to popular belief, the Church Commissioners are in no way responsible for cathedrals, which have to rely on their own often slender endowments and the offerings of visitors and friends. In France and elsewhere the state looks after the major cathedrals, but no acceptable formula for this has yet been evolved in Britain.

ARCHITECTURAL GLOSSARY

To avoid unnecessary repetition, page and illustration numbers are quoted wherever possible so that explanations may be found in the main text.

Aisle (p. 15)   Part of a church alongside the nave, quire or transept, usually lower and narrower (*9*).

Ambulatory (p. 18)   The processional way around the inside of a church, especially around the altar (*188*).

Apse (p. 17)   A semi-circular termination, usually behind an altar (*2*). The adjective is apsidal.

Arcade (p. 19)   A row of arches on columns or piers (*6*).

Boss (p. 31) (*43*).

Buttress (p. 22)   A mass of masonry projecting from a wall to give it stability (*34*). A flying buttress stands clear of the wall to resist the thrust of a vault (*182*).

Capital   The head of a column, usually carved or moulded (*12-15*).

Censing angel (*52*)   A figure of an angel distributing incense.

Chancel   The part of a church containing the altar, priest's desk, etc. – not usually applied to cathedrals.

Chantry (p. 39)   A small memorial chapel endowed for saying masses (*92*).

Chapter House (p. 15) (*90*).

Chevet (p. 18) (*194*).

Choir (p. 15).

Cinquefoil (p. 33)   A five-lobed tracery pattern (*31*).

Clerestory (p. 19)   Windows at high level over an arcade (*21*).

Cloister (p. 12) (*89*).

Corbel   A stone projecting from a wall, usually for the support of a roof member (*62*).

196

Corona (*244*) A circular eastern termination to a church or cathedral.

Crocket A hook-like projection, often in the form of a springing leaf (*68*).

Crossing (p. 15) (*Front endpaper*)

Cruciform Cross-shaped: applied to church plans with transepts (*130, 131*).

Cusp (p. 31) (*33*).

Diaper (p. 41) A repetitive ornament, usually based on a square grid (*55*).

Dormitory (p. 12) A communal sleeping apartment (*154*).

Finial (*53*) A termination of, for example, a gable or a spire.

Font (p. 78) A ceremonial basin for baptism (*97*).

Frater (*109*) A monastery refectory or dining-hall.

Galilee A western porch enlarged into the form of a chapel (*113*).

Garth (*117*) A garden court, such as that of a cloister.

Grisaille (p. 31).

Groin (p. 19) A vault-junction without a rib (*9*).

Hall-church A church with aisles of the same height as the nave.

Lady Chapel A chapel for the special worship of Our Lady, often at the extreme E end of a cathedral (*135*).

Lantern Tower A tower with high-level windows over the surrounding roofs, lighting the space beneath (*231*).

Lierne (p. 35) (*43*).

Loggia A recessed wall-arcade or gallery.

Lunette (*76*) An arched opening in the side of a ceiling.

Misericord (p. 71) (*95*).

Mouldings The continuous projecting and recessed contours of arches and other architectural members (*22*).

Mullion A vertical post separating the 'lights' of a window (*49*).

Narthex A western compartment of a church, larger than a porch and similar to a galilee (*225*).

Nave (p. 15) (*Front endpaper*).

Niche A recess for a statue (*68, 69*).

Ogee (p. 35) (*53*).

Pendentive (*185*) One of the triangular spandrels leading from a round dome down to a square base.

Pier A mass of masonry supporting a section of a building and not necessarily forming part of a wall (*4*).

Pinnacle A small spiky vertical projection, either ornamental or placed as a holding-down weight on top of a buttress (*64, 182*).

Podium (*165*) A base or platform on which a building stands.

Presbytery (p. 15) As well as meaning the part of a church where a priest officiates (*front endpaper*), this word is applied by Roman Catholics to a priest's residence.

Pro-cathedral A church serving as a cathedral, i.e. housing the bishop's throne, pending the erection of a permanent building.

Pulpitum (p. 67) A screen at the W end of a quire (Pl. E). A **Jubé** is a gallery on top of it.

Quatrefoil (p. 33) A four-lobed tracery pattern (*29*).

Quire (p. 14) (*Front endpaper*).

Refectory (p. 12) A monastic dining hall, also called a frater (*154*).

Reredos (p. 76) A wood, metal or stone construction behind an altar (*87*).

Retro-quire. The part of a cathedral immediately east of, i.e. behind, the altar (*front endpaper*).

Rib (p. 19) (*21*).

Ridge The top of a sloping roof (*182*).

Rood A figure of Our Lord on the cross, a crucifix.

Sanctuary The part of a church immediately surrounding an altar (*front endpaper*).

Slype A dark passage, usually between a transept and chapter-house (*113*).

Spandrel The space left over between two shapes, particularly that between an arch and its surrounding rectangle (*21*).

String-course A projecting horizontal moulding on a wall, either for ornament or to throw water off the face (*41*).

Tabernacle An ornamented niche or canopy.

Tierceron (p. 30) (*58*).

Tracery Stonework patterns in window-heads and elsewhere (*46-49*).

Transept (p. 15) (*Front endpaper*).

Transom A horizontal member separating the upper and lower 'lights' of a window (*66-67*).

Trefoil (p. 33) A three-lobed tracery pattern (*28*).

Tribune (p. 19) (*4*) A gallery over an aisle, sometimes called a triforium.

Triforium (p. 19) (*21*) A small triangular roof space over an aisle, or the arcade screening it.

Tympanum The infilling below an arch and over a flat-headed doorway, especially in Romanesque building (*186*).

Vault An arched construction of masonry usually exposed on its underside, supporting a roof or floor (*42-44*).

Vesica (p. 135) A vertical shape formed by two curves intersecting at points at top and bottom (*171*).

INDEX

SPAIN AND PORTUGAL showing the principal cathedrals

ITALY AND YUGOSLAVIA showing the principal cathedrals

ENGLAND AND WALES showing all cathedrals and some important monastic buildings

- Church of England Cathedrals
- Roman Catholic Cathedrals
- Abbeys, Priories & Collegiate Churches mentioned in the text
- Welsh Cathedrals

Lanercost
Hexham Newcastle
Carlisle Durham
Middlesbrough
Mount Grace Whitby
Cartmel Rievaulx
Furness Lancaster Ripon Byland
Peel Bolton Fountains Bridlington
Kirkstall York
Blackburn Leeds Beverley
Liverpool Bradford Selby
St Asaph Manchester Wakefield Howden
Salford Sheffield
Bangor Chester Worksop Lincoln
Denbigh Wrexham Southwell
Valle Crucis Derby Nottingham Binham
Shrewsbury Buildwas Lichfield Castle Acre North Elmham
Wenlock Crowland Norwich
Birmingham Leicester Peterborough Wymondham
Leominster Coventry Thorney
Strata Worcester Ramsey Bury St Edmunds
Florida Malvern Northampton Ely
Hereford Pershore Colchester
Brecon Dore Tewkesbury Dunstable Chelmsford
Llanthony Deerhurst Gloucester Oxford Waltham
Tintern Malmesbury St Albans Brentwood
Newport Dorchester
Llandaff Clifton Westminster London
Cardiff Wells Bristol Lacock Southwark Canterbury
Downside Bath Old Sarum Winchester Guildford Rochester
Glastonbury Salisbury Bexgrove Arundel
Crediton Wimborne Ramsey Chichester
Ottery Sherborne Portsmouth
St Mary Milton Quarr
Exeter Christchurch
St Germans Plymouth
Truro